Our Elected King, Who Speaks Out!

(It is Time for some Sane Person to get Control of this Insane World!)

By
The Worldwide People's Revolution!®

Book 070 ♦♥★

(A Photo of New York City from the Top of the Empire State Building)

Copyright and Dedication

By
Dr. Samuel Walker Edison, Ph.D., MA., BS, and QC!

ISBN — 13: 978-1539-5691-45
ISBN — 10: 1539-5691-44

This Inspired Book is COPYRIGHTED 2016—4017 AD, by **"The Worldwide People's Revolution!"** All Rights are Reserved for the Truth's Sake. No Portion of this Unique Book shall be Reproduced by any Means for Sale without Written Permission from **The Worldwide People's Revolution!®**, except for the Introduction and Table of Contents, which can be Published by whomever is Willing, whereby they will become Automatic Members of **"The Worldwide People's Revolution!"** However, with our Permission, anyone in the World may Reproduce Exact Copies of this Book, and Sell them for a Reasonable Profit, and Keep 90% of the Net Profits for their own Prosperity: beCause our Elected King only Wants 10% of the Net Profits for the Construction of **"The Great World TEMPLE of PEACE,"** in Jerusalem, which will be the Tallest and Largest Building in the World, being nearly a Mile Tall and 8+ Miles in Diameter, being Built in 60 Great Terraces, with 10 Lesser Terraces within each Great Terrace, within which will be tens of thousands of Stone Dome Home Complexes for the Elected Officials and their Voluntary Servants of **"The New RIGHTEOUS One-World Government!"**

This Inspired Book is now DEDICATED to all of those Elected Officials, their Staffs and their Volunteer Servants, who will consist of one Great Selected King, who has been Selected by God, who is also Elected by 6 High Priests from 6 Major Religions, 60 Elected Righteous Kings from 60 Major Nations, and a Maximum of 600 Elected Governors from Minor Nations and Islands of the Seas, who will be Elected by Qualified Members of **"The Worldwide People's Revolution,"** which Elected Officials will Live and Work within **"The Great World TEMPLE of PEACE,"** in Jerusalem, who will be in Command of **"Seven Great Armies of Working Soldiers,"** who will be Well-Organized and Equipped for the Construction of **"GLORIOUS Swanky Hotels Castles and Fortresses,"** which will Solve no less than 248 Massive Problems, and thousands of Minor Problems: beCause of being **"The Right Design for Living!"** Book 012. Indeed, **"The Swanky Associations of Working Soldiers"** will take on Massive Work Projects, like the World has never Seen before, whereby all People may end up Living within **"Beautiful Swanky PALACES,"** which is **a New Concept in Living Habits — even Swanky Palaces for Poor People!** Therefore, it is now Time to Inform your Friends, Relatives, and Naaberz all about it, by one Means or another, by Sharing this Inspired Book with them, or by making Perfect Copies of *The Introduction* and *Content* Pages, which can be Printed on just 3 Sheets of Paper, which are 11x17-inches. Those Volunteer Working Soldiers (as Opposed to Drafted Working Soldiers) will be Paid According to **"A List of FAIR Swanky Wages!"** Therefore, please Inform your Friends, Relatives, and Naabers about it: beCause they might know someone in this World of Wonders, who Needs some Help in a Riit Waa.

(It is Time for some Sane Person to get Control of this Insane World!)

— The Introduction —

Is by our Selected and Elected King, himself,
Who is a Humble and Honest Man of Great Faith and True Love,
Whose Sword of Truths is not Challenged by anyone on this Earth,
Who is the King of the Mountains by Virtue of the Fact that he
Presents the Most Reasonable Solutions for our Massive Problems,
Whom you will also Agree with, if you have a Riit Miind!

00-01 [_] Hello, my Friend or Enemy. I am the Elected King of **"The Worldwide People's Revolution!"**, which you have probably not Heard of, until now: beCause they have not been Advertising themselves by any Means. In Fact, they are Trusting ME to do that for them, which I am Happy to do: beCause they Represent the Vast Majority of the Happy and Unhappy People in this World of Wonders and Woes, who have Desperately Needed a RIGHTEOUS KING to Govern them, who has Power and Authority that no Elected President, Prime Minister, nor other Elected Official might have, who are generally only Political Puppets on the Strings of Lying Red Jew Bankers, who Control the Money Supply. Therefore, after Studying **"The Complete SURVEYS of our VALUES,"** and especially my own Personal Values, **The Worldwide People's Revolution!®** have Unanimously Agreed that I am most Qualified to be their Elected King, even though I have Protested Against it with very Strong Arguments, even as you would also likely Protest: beCause of the Heavy-duty Responsibilities of such an Office. However, it is now Time for some Sane Person to get Control of this Insane World!

00-02 [_] Therefore, after Voting for one of 2 or 3 or more Right/WRong, Rong/Riit Parties, according to the Standard Election Deception Plan, it is Doubtful that you, nor anyone else, is Well-Pleased by it all. In Fact, at least half of the People did not even Bother themselves to Vote in the last Election Deception, and the other half were Divided about 50/50, and even more Divided concerning the Important Issues of the Day. Indeed, I would venture to say that most of the Electors only Voted on Account of their HOPE that so-and-so might Fix the Mess, and make Things Better for them. However, History Proves that such is seldom if ever the Case in **"The Divided States of United Lies,"** which has a Track Record of more and more DEBTS, Poverty, Obesity, Drug Addicts, Rapes, Mass Shootings, Prisoners, and High-ranking Criminals in Washington, which is otherwise known as "The District of Criminals," "The District of Corruption," or "The District of Columbian Drug Addicts."

00-03 [_] Now, you might be Wondering WHY that I do not Show to you my Face? Well, it is simply beCause of the Need for my Personal Security among Vicious Lions and Mean Bears, you might say, since I do not have 5,000+ Security Guards to Protect me, like the President of Political Rabbits has, which Rabbits come Out of their Stinking Holes every few Years, and Hop all around the Country, and give to us their Repetitious Political Speeches, who have no Reasonable Solutions for anything, even though they do make Various Kinds of PROMISES, which they cannot Keep: beCause it Requires the Cooperation of the CONgress to get anything Done in Washington, D.C., except for making WAR!

00-04 [_] Some of those Lying Deceiving Political Rabbits even Promise to NOT Lie, whom we are supposed to Trust, and also Support with our Freewill Offerings — that is, IF we Like their Childish Solutions, which never go into enough Details to get a Good Picture of whatever they Propose: beCause the Art of Politics is to make the Electors IMAGINE whatever the Missing Pieces of their Political Puzzle might Look like, once they get Elected. Yes, then their Plastic Roses will Bloom with Fragrant and Spectacular Colors, we HOPE! But, our Hope is always in Vain: beCause none of those Political Rabbits have any REAL Workable Solutions for our Massive Problems, which sets me Apart from all of them: beCause I have Guaranteed Solutions, which I Intend to Present within this one Recording for your Enlightenment, Education, and Entertainment, which you are Welcome to Reproduce and Sell for a Reasonable Profit!

00-05 [_] After all, being the Elected King, I would be nothing but another Ignorant FOOL, if I did not Present Reasonable Solutions for ALL of our Massive Problems, after being Elected by **The Worldwide People's Revolution!®**, which Naturally Expects me to Present Solutions that no Sane Person can Challenge, beginning with a much Better Plan for Electing our Officials, which would Require all Potential Leaders to Fill Out and File on the Internet **"The Complete SURVEYS our VALUES,"** even **SURVEYS of Religious Spiritual Political Governmental Sexual Social Moral Economic Business Labor Habitual and Miscellaneous VALUES**, whereby we might all Study such Surveys, and then Rationally Decide **"WHO QUALIFIES to Rule Over US,"** rather than Deceive ourselves with another Election Deception, whereby we have no Real Idea just Exactly what those Political Candidates have in their Heads, nor in their Hearts, who may very well be Related with Snakes, Wolves in Sheep's Clothing, and even Chief Hypocriters, if ye knoweth what I Meaneth, as Nigger Jim might say to Huck Finn in *"The Adventures of Judge Thatcher,"* by Mark Twain, who was one of the most Honest Authors, who would likely have much to Say about Modern Political Maneuverings, if he were here, Today. After all, Mark Twain was a very Observant Person, who Judged that the only Difference between a Rattlesnake and a Politician is the Fact that the Politician is Missing his Rattles, whereby we might be Warned about his Poisonous Fangs; but, other than that, such Colorful Snakes seem to be very Attractive to many People: beCause of Various Reasons, which I will not bother myself to Explain at this Time: beCause we have much more Important Issues to Address and Think about with a Capital T.

00-06 [_] First of all, unlike those Wicked Politicians, I am now coming right up Front to Confess with a Good Conscience that I am about to tell some Lies to you, just to Offend those Poisonous Snakes, who might like to Strike Back at me, who are Hiding among the Bushes with Little Dick Chicanery, if you know what I Mean. Yes, the Woods are Full of those Poisonous Snakes in Various Colors and Kinds, who simply cannot be Trusted. Moreover, I am not Asking anyone to Trust *me,* neither: beCause I am Forced to tell a few Harmless Lies, just for my own National Securities' Sake, even as Jesus Christ told his Parables for the very same Reason, which Required TIME for those Wicked Scribes and Pharisees to Figure those Parables Out, which gave to Jesus enough Time to Escape from them, which was True Wisdom on his Part, even as it is Wise of me to Camouflage my own Tale of Truths, whereby I can also Hide myself in this Concrete Jungle. After all, I am already Wanted by the Federal Burden of Investigation (FBI), and the Central Unintelligent Agencies (CIA), as well as other High-ranking Criminals in Washington: beCause they do not like the Sound of **The Worldwide People's Revolution!®** — much less the Idea that they might also have to Fill Out and File **"The Complete SURVEYS our VALUES,"** on the Internet for Honest People to Study. Yes, it could Prove to be very Em-

(It is Time for some Sane Person to get Control of this Insane World!)

BARE-assing, as my Daddy used to say, which would get a LOT of "Amens" and "Hallelujahs" from the Electors, even if they were Atheists at Heart, who have no Real Proof that the Hebrew God even Exists!

00-07 [_] However, we can all be Sure that a Great Creator God does Exist, and that he Created all GOOD Things, including at least one BAD Thing, called the Devil, himself: beCause he is very Useful for Testing our Spirits and Minds, whereby the Creator God might Decide whether or not any of us are Worthy to Govern in his Countless Worlds, which are still Multiplying, even as the Birds of the Air and the Fishes in the Seas: beCause it is a Universal LAW that every Living Thing should Multiply, which is also GOOD, even if they are those Hateful Mosquitoes with their Viruses, which also have Good Lessons to Teach to us — one of which is the Fact that Satan is Alive and Insane, who even Vainly Imagines that he will some Day Conquer God, and thus take Over his Glorious Kingdom. Nevertheless, that is another Subject that I must Address during the Future, which really has nothing to do with this Speech, which is all about Reasonable Solutions for our Massive Problems. I Trust that you have the Patience to Hear me out to the End: beCause I Present some really GOOD News.

00-08 [_] Now, I Hear someone, who is like a Workhorse without a Harness, whinny: "O Elected King, I got my College Degree in Mental Rapeology, and Graduated with a Master's Degree in Philosophy; but, at no Time did I Learn just HOW a Righteous KING could make it Possible for almost everyone in the World to become Moderately RICH, and without Telling any Lies, nor Selling any Trash. Therefore, would you mind Explaining that to us Tax Slaves, Interest Slaves, Insurance Slaves, Drug Slaves, Sex Slaves, Childcare Slaves and Work Slaves, in such a Way that even a 12-year-old Child might Understand it?" {See: **"LIGHTNING Versus the Lig ..."**}

00-09 [_] Well, O Workhorse, I See that you have done a lot of Sweating in the Fields of the Devil, and are now Stuck in a Rut, in the Tar Pits of Poverty, you might say, which you cannot easily get Out of: beCause of being Burdened Down with seemingly "Endless" Debts. Yes, you are getting Older and less Patient than ever. However, if you can muster up the Patience to Hear me out, you will be Running and Jumping for sheer JOY! Therefore, if you do not get the Message LOUD and Clear the first Time around, then just Play this DVD Message to some Friend, who might Help you to Understand it: beCause not everyone has the same Education, much less the same Wisdom and Good Understanding, as King Solomon might say. {FOOT-NOTE: If you are a Good Reader, you have my Permission to make up your own Exact DVD Recording of this Message, and Publish it, just to Tease the Federal Burden of Investigation and the Central Unintelligent Agencies, if nothing else, whereby they will not be Able to Track me down, and Assassinate me for Publishing **"The Swanky Sword of Divine Truths!"** and **"The Great Worldwide TELEVISED Court HEARING!"** After all, it is Physically Possible for almost everyone in the World to become Moderately RICH, and without Telling any Lies, nor Selling any Trash.} However, before we get into the Details about that, let us Consider a few little Truths with Great Implications, which have long been Neglected by the Elite Class of educated Fools, who have more than 20 Different Ways to Spell the single Sound of "OO," as in Sch**oo**l, r**u**le, d**o**, sh**oe**, thr**ough**, fr**ui**t, cr**ew**, man**eu**ver, Si**oux** (as in Sq Indians), tw**o**, bl**ue**, **rhu**barb, **rheu**matism, rendezv**ous**, gh**ou**l, l**ieu**, and p**oo**h!

00-10 [_] So, O Elected King, are you saying that we could spell the "OO" Sound with only one Letter, as in "Q"? Therefore, school would be S-K-Q-L, and rule would be R-Q-L, and do would be D-Q, and through would be T-H-R-Q, etcetera, etc. Is it any Wonder that X-amount of little Children cannot Learn HOW to read and write: beCause of the Inconsistencies of our Spelling Rules?

00-11 [_] Yes, that is Exactly what I am saying, whereby we could Save X-amount of Years of Needless Spelling Lessons in **"The Public School of IGNERUNT FQLZ!"** {See my Inspired Book, called: **"Are you a Jobless Graduate of the SKQL uv FQLZ?" (HOW to get a GOUD EJUKAASHUN without Robbing the Bank!) By The Worldwide People's Revolution!®**}

00-12 [_] God have Mercy, O Elected King, why did the Founding Fathers not Think of that?

00-13 [_] Well, they were likely too Busy trying to figure out HOW to Enrich their own Bank Accounts, rather than Think about True Prosperity for everyone, which would Begin with a Good Education with a Capital G and E. Indeed, you probably have Heating and Cooling Bills to Pay; but, I do NOT: beCause of taking Advantage of my Nolij, which is one of the Major Reasons WHY **The Worldwide People's Revolution!®** has Elected me to be their RIGHTEOUS King, which you will no doubt also Conclude is the Best Way to Go, after coming to the next Crossroad in your Life, whereby you will have to Decide to Turn RIIT or Left, or just keep on going in the same Insane Direction as you and the whole Society of Ignorant Fools have been Going! (Yes, many Proud People will no doubt be Offended by such a Statement: beCause of Judging that they are NOT Fools, even though they will have to Confess that it might be Financially Better for them to not have any Heating nor Cooling Bills — not to Mention how much Pollution could be Cut Off by simply having a Proper House to Live in.) {See my Inspired Book, called: **"Are we Americans the Most STUPID People who ever Lived?" (HOW Working People can PROSPER and Live in PEACE Under the Rulership of a RIGHTEOUS KING!) By The Worldwide People's Revolution!®**}

00-14 [_] Now, you must Try to Remember that I come from a Different World than yours, which has ZERO Pollution: beCause everyone uses Wind- and Solar-powered Electric Elevators and Subway Trains for Transportation, whereby no one has any Need for Airplanes, Cars, Vans, Pickups, Trucks, Buses, Tractors, Lawnmowers, Garden Tillers, Motorcycles, Motor Scooters, Motorboats, Weed-eaters, Leaf Blowers, Chainsaws, nor any other Noisy Stinking Polluting Abominations, much less any Need for those Atomic-Powered ElecTrickery Plants with their Radioactive Dung, which should be Fed to the Wicked Federal Government Officials, until they come to their Riit Senses. After all, it is Possible and most Practical for almost everyone to Live within Beautiful Planned City States, each of which Governs itself, according to its own Elected Laws and Flexible Rules, whereby the People who are like Sheeps and Goats can be Separated from the People who are like Lions and Wolves, whereby they can all Live with Like-minded People in PEACE with True Prosperity.

00-15 [_] Now, I Hear someone, who is like a Confused Sheep of the Good Shepherd, bleat: "O Elected King, are you Suggesting that we were not all Born Equal, whereby we should not have Equal RIGHTS to Live with whomever we might Want to Live?"

00-16 [_] Well, O Sheep, would you Willingly Choose to Live in a House with Rats and Mice and Snakes and Skunks running all about, when you could Choose to put Doors and Screened Windows on the House, just to Keep OUT all such Unwanted Varmints? Indeed, you could

(It is Time for some Sane Person to get Control of this Insane World!)

Invite all of those Varmints into your House of Hate, and then Tax yourself to take Good Care of them; or, you could simply Wall them OUT! Therefore, I would not Invite anyone into my Beautiful Planned City State, until that Person should Fill Out and File **"The Complete SURVEYS of our VALUES,"** whereby I might Discover whether or not such a Person might be Worthy to Live with Law-abiding Trustworthy People, like myself, whereby I might Live in Peace with them. For Example, which ones of the following Boxes would you Check with an X, which have the Statements that you Agree with?

A-[_] I Promise to not Steal anything from my Naaberz: beCause I would not Want my Naaberz Stealing anything from me. Remember the Golden Rule, to *"Do unto others as you would have others do unto you." — One of the Sayings of Jesus Christ.*

B-[_] I Prefer to Buy Locks for all of my Doors, and put Steel Prison Bars on all of my Windows, and Hope to God that no one Discovers how to get into my House of Hate when I am on a Swankless Vacation with my Aunt Polly and the Widow Douglas. §

C-[_] I Prefer to Hire a Security Guard, who stands around with nothing Constructive to do, which is Extremely Boring, whereby he might become Depressed, or even Trigger Happy after Consuming some Medically-approved Drugs to Relieve his Depression. §§

D-[_] I Prefer that Corporations are Taxed for Hiring Security Guards for everyone within Cities of Confusion. Yes, DUMBmocracy can now Vote for it.

E-[_] Educated People have no Use for Fools: because they have been Enlightened in **"The Public School of IGNERUNT FQLZ!"** — who cannot even Spell NOLIJ without using an extra K, W, D, G and 2 extra E's, as in k-n-o-w-l-e-d-g-e! †§‡

F-[_] I Fail to Understand what this Funny Survey is all about.

G-[_] God knows that you Desperately Need some True Education with a Capital T and E, which can only be Obtained in the Unholy Church of Graceful Sinners and Lying Hypocrites. †§‡§§

H-[_] HUMBUG! I will let the Police take Good Care of those Thieves, which is WHY that I Pay my Taxes: so that I might be Free and Happy, even though I will Confess that it is Possible to Live without any Thieves, Liars, Robbers, Rapists, Murderers, Drug Addicts, Swindlers, nor any other Criminals, who can be Discovered and Banished from our Beautiful Planned City States. †§‡

I-[_] I am an Innocent Lamb of God, who would like to Remain this Way; but, you People seem to be Determined to make me into another Child of Hell, like yourselves. Otherwise, Mothers would be able to Stay at Home and Raise their own Baby Jesuses. {See: **"GOOD NEWS for REBEL WOMEN!" (HOW almost all Wives can become Moderately RICH, without Leaving their Homes! Guaranteed!) By The Worldwide People's Revolution!®** Book 010, which has a very Special Chapter 04.}

J-[_] Justice Demands that you should have the Right and Assistance to Maintain your Innocence, which can only be Done by Electing **"The New RIGHTEOUS One-World Government!" (HOW to Establish a Righteous One-World Government without Going to WAR!) By The Worldwide People's Revolution!® Book 056.**

K-[_] King Jesus would Object to that Plan: because he has Plans for Establishing his *own* Righteous One-World Government, called *the Kingdom of God.* Yes, read your Unholy Mutilated Bible for the Proof, which is Missing several Important Books. †§‡§§

L-[_] Lots of Laughs! King Jesus has had more than 2,000 Years to Establish his Righteous One-World Government, if he were Interested in it; but, no Sane Person, including Jesus Christ, would be Interested in being the King of such an Insane World as this, which could End with a Great Atomic Nightmare — Thanks to Demon-ocracy! †§‡

M-[_] If you Pay to me enough Money, I will be your Righteous King, and I will Cut Taxes for the Rich People: so that they will have more Money for Hiring more Tax Slaves, Interest Slaves, Insurance Slaves, Drug Slaves, Sex Slaves, Childcare Slaves, and Work Slaves to be Paid Minimum Wages, whereby they can Barely Survive from Paycheck to Paycheck, and Retire in Subway Sewage Systems, until they Die from one of 300,000+ Diseases: beCause of not having ObamaScare Healthcare Insurance. †§‡§§

N-[_] Thank God that not everyone is as Crazy as you are, O Sarcastic Nitwit. Remember the American Bisons, who Roamed on the Great Plains for thousands of Years without any of those Hateful Diseases, Drugs, Medical Doctors, nor Unsanitary Hospitals. {See www.Amazon.com for: **"Did God or Satan Ordain Medical Doctors??" (Ask Huck Finn and/or Nigger Jim: because neither Tom Sawyer nor Judge Thatcher would Know!) By The Worldwide People's Revolution!® Book 022.**}

O-[_] Are there no Options to Choose from? Must we Vote for a Dimwitcrat or Reprobate, only? Whatever Happened to the Independent Jackasses? {See: **"The Low Court of Supreme Injustices is Brought to Trial!" (The Worldwide People's Revolution!® Butts Heads with the United States Supreme Court, with or without their Black Robes of Hypocrisies and Lies!)**, which contains the Famous *Declaration of Interdependence,* and the Proper Wording for the Placard on the Statue of Liberty. See also: **"The UGLY Scarred Dishonest Face of Poor Old Miserable UNCLE SAM!" (A Memorial Day Legacy!) By The Worldwide People's Revolution!® Book 054.**}

P-[_] Most People cannot Understand all such Inspired Words of Provable Truths: beCause they are Extremely POOR, being in a State of Mental Poverty, Physical Poverty, Financial Poverty, Material Poverty, Diplomatic Poverty, and Spiritual Poverty, being Poor Wretched and Miserable without even Realizing it! (See *Revelation 3, Gay King James Version.*)

Q-[_] The Great Question is this: **"Have we Tax Slaves Suffered Long Enough to come to our Riit Senses; or, must we go on Suffering for another thousand Years, being Under the Bad Administration of Lying Red Jews?"** Indeed, it is now Time to Elect a RIGHTEOUS and HONEST White Jew, like Jesus Christ, who can Set the Household in

Order for his Second Coming. {See: **"Are we Tax Slaves of a Lower Order than Lying Red JEWS?" (HOW to be Liberated from all Slavery, Worldwide!) By The Worldwide People's Revolution!®**, Book 052, which is a Companion Book of: **"The Loathsome Burdens of the Independent Jackasses!" (A New Approach for Solving our Massive Problems!)**, Book 051, which is a Companion Book of: **"The Great False Economy is now DEBUNKED!" (Adolf Hitler had a much Better Economic System!) By The Worldwide People's Revolution!®** Book 053.}

R-[_] Has the Resurrected Christ already Returned? Is he your Elected King, O Rebels?

S-[_] Satan has all of you People Greatly Deceived, Drugged, and Drunk with Red Jew Propagandist LIES! For Example, you Claim to be Free, while in Reality you are nothing but Tax Slaves, Interest Slaves, Insurance Slaves, Debt Slaves, Drug Slaves, and Work Slaves, who should be Stripped of your Pride, and Forced to Prove in a Courtroom that any of you are Free with a Capital F, and thus be Sentenced to DEATH, if you cannot Prove it, and Refuse to Accept the one and only Reasonable Solution for these Massive Problems, which is to Establish **"The New RIGHTEOUS One-World Government!"**

T-[_] Tally-Ho, Mates, it is now Time for another REVOLUTION, and a Worldwide Bloodless Revolution, whereby all of the Tax Slaves just STAY IN BED, and Refuse to get up and do anything, until the Leaders of all Nations Present themselves at: **"The Great Worldwide TELEVISED Court HEARING,"** at which Time our Elected King will Ask them a few very Important Questions, which they will not be Able to Answer: beCause of being Born and Raised in the DARK Loathsome Prison of Red Jew LIES, in the Darkness of Ignorance, where the Bright Lights of Pure Truths seldom Shine! †§‡

U-[_] I Understand the Meanings of all of those Words; but, I do not Understand the Figures of Speech, which are Mysterious to me, being a Grade School Dropout, who is otherwise known as the Utopian Child of Hell, whose Father and Mother are Spiritual COWARDS. Nevertheless, I Promise to Keep on Listening and Learning: because I am Enticed by those **"Beautiful Swanky PALACES!" (A New Concept in Living Habits — Swanky Palaces for Poor People!) By The Worldwide People's Revolution!®**

V-[_] Queen Victoria would Envy us for such Beautiful Palaces with their Luscious All-Mineral Organic Gardens. {See www.Amazon.com for: **"The LUSCIOUS All-Mineral Organic Method of Gardening!" (HOW to Grow DELICIOUS Satisfying Foods for Potential Kingz and Kweenz in Swanky PALACES!) By The Worldwide People's Revolution!®** Book 021.}

W-[_] I would rather go to WAR, than to Submit to any Elected King, even if he were as Righteous as Jesus Christ, himself: beCause Men cannot be Trusted, much less Wombmen, who have Mood Swings, which can Change with the Weather. †§‡

X-[_] X-amount of Ignorant People will Naturally Agree with you. However, our Elected King has a Track Record that cannot be Beat! Yes, he is a VIRGIN, if you can Believe it, who has no Criminal Record, who also has no Pains within his entire Body, who has not used any Drugs of any Kind during his entire Life, in spite of being Forced in the Army to get Shots of Puss, contrary to his own Will, which was more than 50 Years Ago. Therefore, he can be Trusted with the Royal British Crowns and Jewels. †§‡

Y-[_] I Yearn for the Happy Day when all Provable Truths are Proven at: **"The Great Worldwide TELEVISED Court HEARING!" (That Great Meeting of the Most Intelligent Minds!)** Yes, that will be a Time of Great Rejoicing among all Righteous People, Worldwide.

Z-[_] The Zeal of **The Worldwide People's Revolution!®** will make that Possible and most Practical for Solving our Massive Problems.

00-17 [_] So, O Elected King, does your Holy City not have any Thieves in it? What about Rapists and Murderers? {See www.Amazon.com for: **"The Secret City of the Great King!" (HOW the True Church will Escape from the Great Tribulation!) By The Worldwide People's Revolution!®** Book 042.}

00-18 [_] Well, if a Bad Person is Discovered, he or she is simply Banished from the City, if he or she cannot be Corrected; and therefore, there are no Criminals within that Holy City.

00-19 [_] O King, I find that Difficult to Believe. Nevertheless, I would like to Learn about those Self-air-conditioned Houses, which have no Heating nor Cooling Bills.

00-20 [_] Well, when the Walls and Roof of the House are a Minimum of 10 feet THICK, neither the Heat nor the Cold can Penetrate through them. Therefore, it Pays to have THICK Solid Stone Walls on all Rooms, which have Solid Stone Domes, or Concrete Domes with Skylight Vents, which Rooms are Joined by Barrel-vault Tunnels, which Skylights are used to Control the Air Flow: because of having Windows that can be Opened or Closed, much like Saint Peter's Basilica, in Rome, which has no Air-conditioning System, other than Windows and Doors, which are Opened or Closed by the Managers. Likewise, the Pantheon in Rome is Self-air-conditioned, which has Saved the Romans Millions of Dollars during the past 1,800+ Years.

00-21 [_] O Elected King, I must Confess that your House-building Plan is Superior to any Houses in America; but, WHO could Afford such Well-made Houses?

00-22 [_] Well, with a Righteous King in Charge, everyone in the World can Afford such Well-made Houses: beCause the Mountains of Rocks are FREE to Harvest them, which would Require less Energy than running around on Endless Highways, while Wasting Billions of Gallons of Gasoline per Day, while Polluting the Atmosphere with Abominations, which cause Acid Rains, which Weaken the Trees and Plants, making them Susceptible to all Kinds of Diseases, which Inspire Ignorant Fools to use Various Kinds of Harmful Sprays and Poisons, which Cause Cancers and whatever — Thanks to that Great False Economic Goddess with the 12 Leaking Breasts, called: CAPITALISM, which is the Love of Money in Action, which God HATES: beCause it is the Root Cause for almost all Evils! (See *First Timothy 6,* for the Proof.)

00-23 [_] O Elected King, how in the World would we get to Work, if we did not have Cars and other Vehicles to Ride in?

(It is Time for some Sane Person to get Control of this Insane World!)

00-24 [_] Well, if you were Wise, you would get up and go to Work in your own Home-craft Workshop, or Luscious All-Mineral Organic Garden, Vineyard, and Orchard, where you could Grow most of your own Foods — that is, IF you had a Righteous King to Help you to get Set Up Properly for Living with a Capital L, which would Require at least 3 feet of Rich Topsoil in the Garden, which would be directly in front of your Stone Dome Home Complex, and on the Roof of the Family who Lives below you in their Stone Dome Home Complex: beCause all of the Cities will be Built in Great TERRACES, whereby all of the Roofs will be Covered with Gardens, which will Save hundreds of Trillions of Dollars during the Future: beCause of not Needing to Travel very far to get to Work. {See www.Amazon.com for: **"The Right Design for Living!" (A List of Great Advantages for Building Beautiful Planned City States!)**, Book 012, plus: **"Poverty Hunger Riots Strikes Brutalities Election Deceptions and Civil Wars!" (The High Price that we Earthlings have Paid for Leaving the Good Land!)**, Book 014, plus: **"GLORIOUS Swanky Hotels Castles and Fortresses!" (Beautiful Planned City States for WISE Intelligent Well-Educated People with Common Sense and Good Understanding!) By The Worldwide People's Revolution!®** Book 019.}

00-25 [_] So, O Elected King, are you saying that there never was any Need for Poverty in this World of Woes? Why did Jesus Christ not Explain a few Things to us Tax Slaves?

00-26 [_] Well, he was a Holy Prophet, who Knew that I would come along and Explain all such Things to you, which is just one of the many Wonderful Things that you will Learn from me, if you Listen Carefully, and do not Allow any Lady Doubtfulness to Discourage you by any Means. Indeed, one of our Worst Enemies is Unbelief. Therefore, keep an Open Mind, and be Willing to Learn New Lessons: beCause I have very Good News for you to Learn, which you should Share with your Friends, Relatives, Naaberz, and even with your so-called "Enemies," if they have any Interest in it: beCause that is what you would Want other People to do for you, if they Discovered some really Good News, which might Save the World from the Madness of Greedy Selfish Noisy HOGS, who could care less how much you might Suffer in a State of Ignorance and Extreme Poverty. After all, Fortunately or Unfortunately, it is a "Dog-eat-Dog" World at this Time; but, **The Worldwide People's Revolution!®** has Good Intentions of Overthrowing the Evil Empire, and Establishing **"The New RIGHTEOUS One-World Government,"** which will Mint and Print the Necessary New Money with New Faces and Numbers — NOT to Give it away to Ignorant Fools, nor to Lazy Sloths; but, in Order to Use that New Money WISELY, in Order to HIRE **"Seven Great Armies of Working Soldiers,"** in Order to Voluntarily Help Build those **"GLORIOUS Swanky Hotels Castles and Fortresses,"** which are Designed for True Prosperity, whereby each Family is made Moderately RICH, without Telling any Lies, nor Selling any Trash: beCause, once your Stone Dome Home Complex is Finished, you will be Welcome to Move into it, whereby you are already Moderately RICH — Thanks to the Assistance of Mechanical SLAVES, which will do most of the Hard Work for us, Free of Charges!

00-27 [_] So, O Elected King, are you saying that a Righteous Government would Realize the Need for everyone in the World to have a GOOD Secure House, like the Pantheon, in Rome, which would have at least one Large Cistern, which holds at least a Million Gallons of Water, which is used to Water the Garden when there is Insufficient Rainwater?

00-28 [_] Yes, that is Exactly what I am saying, except that 4 Million Gallons of Water is 4 Times Better than one Million: beCause there is no Guarantee from God nor Government that it will always go on Raining. Therefore, it is Wise to have an Abundance of Fresh Pure Living Water without any Chlorine. Moreover, 2 of those **"Seven Great Armies of Working Soldiers"** would be Producing the Tools for everyone to Work with, whereby each Family could have its own Well-made Tools for Gardening, as well as Special Tools in their Home-craft Workshops, whereby they can Produce those Products that are Needed for True Prosperity, without any Loans, without any Interest, and without any Taxes: beCause everyone Agrees to Learn, Believe, Love, and OBEY **"The New MAGNIFIED Version of the Ten Commandments!"** Yes, that will Eliminate the Need for Policemen, Courtrooms, Judges, Lawyers, Prisons, and Taxes.

00-29 [_] Now, I Hear someone, who is like a Rebel Woman, say: "O Unrighteous King, I have 3 Children, and one of them is a Born Rebel, like myself, who would never Consent to Learning those Ten Commandments, let alone Obeying them: beCause of Wanting his Freedom to Fornicate with his Girlfriend, and also Smoke some Marijuana. Moreover, I am Happily Divorced from my Tyrannical Husband, who was a Religious Fanatic, much like yourself, who Wanted us to Live by the Laws of Moses, which were Crucified with Christ, and thus done away with, if I am reading my Bible Correctly." †§‡

00-30 [_] Well, it Sounds as if you Belong to the Graceful Sinner's Church on Lonesome Street and Suicide Avenue, where Drink-it and Nag-it attend Weekly Services with Innocence, I-Believe, and Giving, who have now become Addiction, Unbelief, and Mischief, as John Bunyan might say in *"The Pilgrim's Progress from this World to that which is to Come."* Yes, you are Lost in the Darkness of Ignorance, along with Billions of other Ignorant People, who do not Realize just how EXTREMELY POOR that you are, who do not even have Fresh Clean Air to Breathe, Pure Living Water to Drink, Wholesome Natural Foods to Eat, Natural Clothing to Wear, nor Secure Houses to Live in, much less Eternal Employment with Good Swanky Wages! {See: **"A List of FAIR Swanky Wages!" (The Equitable Wage System!) By The Worldwide People's Revolution!® Book 065.**}

00-31 [_] So, O Elected King, will those Stone Dome Homes not become DARK DANK MUSTY MOLDY Places to Live: beCause of Sucking in the Humidity in such Horrible Places to Live in, as in the Deep South, in **"The Divided States of United Lies!" (The so-called "United States of North America" in Disguise!)**, Book 058?

00-32 [_] Well, each Stone Dome Home Complex in such Humid Climates must have an ICE HOUSE Under it, which is used Wisely for Sucking Out the Moisture from the House, by Opening a Protected Hatch in the Floor, which Ice can also be used by the Naaber who Lives below you in his Terrace. Moreover, the Melted Ice Water must be Drained into a Coldwater Cistern below the Ice House, which Water is used for making more Ice during the Winter Months, by Pumping it up to the Roof of the Top Terrace from the Bottom Terrace, and into Stainless Steel Ice Trays, which are about 20 feet Long, 20-inches Wide, and 4-inches Deep, which are Set Up in the Garden Spaces for Winter Months, which have Hydraulic Jacks under the Ice Trays, which are used for Running the Ice into Chutes, which Deliver the Ice to the Ice Houses, which can also be used for Cooling the Houses, if they get too Hot during Summer Months.

(It is Time for some Sane Person to get Control of this Insane World!)

00-33 [_] So, O Elected King, how do you Propose that we keep the Raccoons and Rats Out of our Corn Patches? Will each Person have to Build his own Private Swanky Fortress, just to Live in Peace? Moreover, I have Discovered that if the Corn Seeds are Planted when the Moon is Decreasing to a New Moon, the Cobs of Corn will be Hanging Downward, instead of Standing Upward, which helps to keep the Rainwater from Spoiling the Tips of the Corn Cobs, and also makes it Possible to Treat the "Hairs" of the Corn Cobs with Unscented Mineral Oil, which Deters the Moths that lay their Eggs there, which keeps the Worms Out of the Corn. Indeed, just a couple Drops of Oil on the Hairs when they first appear will do the Trick. ‡ (See 00-16-V.)

00-34 [_] Well, each Planned City State must have a Large MOAT around it, which has a Slick Polished Granite Wall on the Inside of the Moat, which Prevents any Snake, Mouse, Rat, Rabbit, Skunk, Opossum, Raccoon, Squirrel, Groundhog, Armadillo, Deer, Bear, Lion, Thief, Rapist, Murderer, Drug Pusher, Robber, or any other Unwanted Creatures from Entering into the City State, including Tax Masters, Usury Masters, and other Greedy Selfish Hogs, which are not Needed for True Prosperity, as Jesus and the Apostle Paul would say.

00-35 [_] Are you saying, O King, that we can all Live Happily without those Squirrelly Bankers and other Loan Sharks?

00-36 [_] Yes, that is Exactly what I am saying: beCause, if anything Needs Doing, **"The New RIGHTEOUS One-World Government"** will Gladly Help us to Do it, without any Loans, without any Interest, and without any Taxes!

00-37 [_] So, O Elected King, if there are no Taxes, WHO will Pay the Wages of those Elected Officials of **"The New RIGHTEOUS One-World Government!"**?

00-38 [_] Well, the Masses of People will Love that Good Government so much that they will just Cheerfully Donate whatever Money is Needed for Feeding and Clothing them, which is known in Biblical Terms as a TITHE or FREEWILL OFFERING — except that **"The Swanky Association of Professional Gardeners"** will take Care of their Foods; and **"The Swanky Association of Clothes Makers"** will take Care of their Clothing, even as they will Do for all of **"The Swanky Associations of Working Soldiers,"** who will Cheerfully Volunteer to do an Average of only 3 Hours of Skilled Common Labor, or 4 Hours of Unskilled Common Labor per Day, or the Equivalent thereof, in Exchange for Living in their **"Beautiful Swanky PALACES!"** Yes, all of the Volunteer Working Soldiers will get to Live in their own **"Beautiful Swanky PALACES,"** just for their Cooperation with their Elected King, who will Cheerfully Do whatever they are Asked to Do: beCause they will all be Living like Kings and Queens in those Palaces, which will also have Schools with Swanky Truth-braries (as Opposed to Public LIE-braries), Churches, Mosques, Synagogues, Temples, Cathedrals, Theaters, Gymnasiums, Tennis Courts, Indoor Swimming Pools, Bowling Alleys, Ice-skating Rinks, Roller-skating Rinks, Concert Halls, Auditoriums, Conference Rooms, and whatever they Want to Work for: beCause of Electing **"The New RIGHTEOUS One-World Government!"** {See: **"The CONSTITUTION for the New RIGHTEOUS One-World GovernMint!" (HOW all Peoples can get True Justice, and Celebrate the Great Year of JUBILEE!)**, Book 016, which is a Companion Book of: **"The Great World TEMPLE of PEACE!"** (The Glory of Jerusalem Arises Again!) By The Worldwide People's Revolution!® Book 017.}

00-39 [_] God have Mercy, O Elected King! How come we did not Think of that 200 Years Ago?

00-40 [_] Well, they did not have the Correct Mechanical Slaves to Work with, 200+ Years Ago. Therefore, it was Impractical for them; but, now we can all go to Work for those Good Swanky Wages — Installing the Polished Marble Tiles on the Solid Stone Walls of our own Swanky Stone Dome Home Complexes, and the Stonework will Represent that New Money, which will have to be Earned by Honest Labor, without any Loans, without any Interest, and without any Taxes, which will make it the very Best Money in all of the World! COPYRIGHTED 2016, by **The Worldwide People's Revolution!**® All Rights Reserved.

The Menu for a Feast of Satisfying Truths!

Chapter 01 — The Bankers are having a Diarrhea of their Minds! ... page 15

Chapter 02 — The Chief Criminals Skip Out of Court ... 20

Chapter 03 — The Perfect Economic System ... 23

Chapter 04 — WHO Qualifies to be the Elected King? ... 26

Chapter 05 — Would a Righteous King Force his Subjects to Believe as he Believes? ... 32

Chapter 06 — Our Elected King Debates the Presidential Candidates ... 35

Chapter 07 — Let the Trumpets Sound! ... 68

Chapter 08 — Shameful Mudslinging Election Campaigns are Coming to an End! ... 71

Chapter 09 — Selected Kings Versus Powerless Presidents! ... 77

Chapter 10 — Fair Warnings! ... 89

Chapters 11—15 will be Supplied after we get some Feedback from our Readers, unless they are Satisfied with this Book just as it is. As of this Date, they are Satisfied.

Chapter 16 — Other Fascinating Literature by the same Inspired Author ... 94

Explanations for Symbols

The Sword Symbol (†) is used after Statements that someone Disagrees with, which may include the Author, himself. The Double Sword of Controversy Symbol (‡) is use after Statements that should be Presented at: **"The Great Worldwide TELEVISED Court HEARING!"** The Sarcasm Symbol (§), or Section Symbol, is used after Sarcastic Statements. 2 such Symbols Represent a DOUBLE Sarcasm, which is so Sarcastic that it Proves itself to be WRong!

(It is Time for some Sane Person to get Control of this Insane World!)

— Chapter 01 —

The Bankers are having a Diarrhea of their Minds!

01-01 [_] Now, you can just Imagine how "Well-Received" all such Information would be among Greedy Selfish Red Jew Bankers, who will most Certainly be put OUT of Business, if I become the Elected King of this Insane World, which presently has more than Seven Billion Extremely Poor People in it, and only a few so-called "Rich" People, none of whom have Fresh Clean Air to Breathe, Pure Living Water to Drink, Wholesome Natural Foods to Eat, nor Secure Houses to Live in, who just Imagine that they are Rich, whose so-called "Riches" could Perish within a Day or 2: beCause they are False Riches, beginning with their Bad Health.

01-02 [_] O Elected King, are you saying that not even the Olympian Athletes are HEALTHY? Is it Possible to have Better Health than they have?

01-03 [_] Well, I will Confess that they have much Better Health than most People; but, they are Certainly NOT as Healthy as the Wild Mountain Goats and Sheeps, who could Leap right over their Heads! In Fact, a Mountain Goat is supposed to be able to Leap Up 20 feet from a Standing Point: because of being so Strong; and they are less than 3 feet Tall, with much Shorter Legs. Moreover, a Rhinoceros can Run for 4 Days, nonstop, they say, which no Man could do, unless he were a HOLY Man. {See: **"HOW to Become a HOLY Man!" (40 Good Reasons WHY People Should FAST and PRAY!) By The Worldwide People's Revolution!® Book 045.**}

01-04 [_] So, O Elected King, are you Able to Run all Day, and not be Weary; and to Walk all Night, and not Faint, as *Isaiah* Reported? — saying: *"Blest are those Wise People who Patiently Wait on the Supreme Ruler by Means of Fasting and Praying: because they shall Renew their Strength. Yes, they shall Mount Up like the Eagles on Wings of Great Faith, you might say, whereby they will be Able to Run all Day long, and not be Weary, and to Walk all Night long, and not Faint."* — The New MAGNIFIED Version (NMV) of *Isaiah* 40:31.

01-05 [_] Well, Thanks to Capitalism, I have been Unable to Accomplish it since 1975, when I was very Strong, after Fasting for 314 Days during 14 Months, after which those Large Rocks were as Light as little Common Bricks. Therefore, I Know that it is Possible, which would especially be Possible for most Young People, and especially for Young Men who have been Raised on Farms and Ranches, who have Good Physical Foundations to Build on, who have mostly Eaten Good Wholesome Natural Foods and Drinks, which would especially be True for the Natives of Poor Countries, who have not been Seduced by the Military Industrial Congressional Bankers' Complex of **"The Divided States of United Lies,"** which has all Kinds of Abominations to Sell to Ignorant People, who have no Idea what they are doing to themselves by Consuming all such Hateful Things, which were Produced to get them Addicted to such Things: so that they might be Sold more of them. Remember the Tobacco Cover-up Crimes, whereby Rich Capitalist Hogs have raked in hundreds of Billions of Dollars from Ignorant Victims of Capitalism, who were not even Warned about the DANGERS of Using such

Products, even as the Candy Makers have no Warning Labels on their Disease-producing Products, which should be Outlawed.

01-06 [_] O Elected King, if you were in Charge of this World of Woes, would you Outlaw the Production and Sales of CANDIES, Cakes, Cookies, and all such Concoctions?

01-07 [_] NO! But, I would Promote the Truth about all such Things, and Present Evidence in Courtrooms Against the Use of them, and also have all Products GRADED, as:

> A-[_] Extremely Good, B-[_] Exceptionally Good, C-[_] Good, D-[_] Fair, E-[_] Poor, F-[_] Bad, and G-[_] Very Bad.

01-08 [_] So, would you not even Allow some Poor Person to Borrow enough Money from some Rich Banker, in order to Build a Candy Factory, using Recycled Used Motor Oil for making Plastic Wrappers for his Candies, which might Contain Lead, Mercury, Arsenic, Cadmium, or some other Toxic Chemicals? Would that be JUSTICE for ALL?

01-09 [_] Well, I Realize that Capitalists are Willing to Say and Do just about anything **"For the Love of Money!"** However, when most People become Moderately RICH, and are Living in **"Beautiful Swanky PALACES,"** they will have no Use for any such Vain Things, much less any Addictions to them: beCause they will have Plenty of Wholesome Natural Sweet Fruits to Eat, which have been Grown by **"The LUSCIOUS All-Mineral Organic Method of Gardening!"** (HOW to Grow DELICIOUS Satisfying Foods for Potential Kingz and Kweenz in Swanky PALACES!) By The Worldwide People's Revolution!® Book 021.

01-10 [_] So, it Sounds as if you Intend to put those Greedy Selfish Red Jew Banksters OUT of Business, O Elected King. Therefore, will they not Hire some Thugs to Assassinate YOU?

01-11 [_] Well, even if they Manage to Murder me, they will not be Able to Destroy **"The Swanky Sword of Divine Truths!" (The Most Powerful Weapon in the Whole Universe!) By The Worldwide People's Revolution!®** Book 067. Therefore, it is nothing to Worry about. Moreover, if they are not Totally Insane, they too will be Happy to Move into their own Swanky Palaces. After all, they were Born and Raised in their Hell-bent Families, who Taught them to Think and Act like Snakes and Squirrelly Bankers. Therefore, they could hardly Help themselves to be Civilized Compassionate Human Beings, who are now Ready to FORGIVE ALL DEBTS, and to Help us to Celebrate the Great Wedding of the Nations! {See www.Amazon.com for: **"The END of CONFUSION!" (The Great CELEBRATION of the Magnificent Wedding of the Humble Honest Nations, and the Grand Year of JUBILEE!) By The Worldwide People's Revolution!®** Book 050.

01-12 [_] O Elected King, I can hardly Believe my Ears! Are you saying that all Bankers in the whole World will just Cheerfully FORGIVE US of ALL DEBTS, even as Moses wrote in *Leviticus 25,* whereby all of the Land will also be Returned to the Masses of People, whereby each Family will Inherit one whole Acre of Land, which is 210 feet by 210 feet, whereby they can Grow their own Foods, and Preserve them in Canning Jars, Walk-in Coolers and Freezers? Will God be Pleased with such Actions, seeing that those Lying Red Jews are his PETS, you might say? †§‡§§

01-13 [_] Well, they are Actually his Enemies, who call themselves Jews; but, in Reality, they are NOT True Israelites by any Means; but, they are Lying RED Jews, who are mostly a Mixture of Israelites and Edomite, whom the Hebrew God HATED for Just Causes: beCause they are mostly LIARS — such as those Scumbag Liars in New Yuck City, who "Created" the Bursting Housing Bubble, whereby they Raked in TRILLIONS of Dollars, while Bankrupting hundreds of millions of People, who were not Aware of their Banker Scams. Therefore, their Bad Actions call for COMPENSATIONS — one of which is the Forgiveness of ALL Debts: beCause God HATES Usury, which makes Poor People Poorer than they already are. (See *Exodus 22:25; and Related Scriptures*. Search for "usury" in the Blue Letter Bible on the Internet. *Romans 9:13*.)

01-14 [_] So, O Elected King, is it Fair to say that you and **The Worldwide People's Revolution!®** are going to make a LOT of very Unhappy JEWS in this World of Woes? Will they not Stir Up another World War, just to Distract our Minds from **"The Swanky Sword of Divine Truths!"**?

01-15 [_] Well, there is a Good Possibility of that: beCause they have Raked in TRILLIONS of Dollars from their Hateful Wars, already — such as the Wars in Afghanistan, Iraq, Vietnam, Korea, Germany, Japan, Libya, Syria, and wherever in the Middle East: beCause they are also the Chief Weapons Manufacturers, Chemical Company Executives, Drug Manufacturers, Medical Doctors, Pharmaceutical Corporations, Movie Makers, and Book Publishers. Indeed, if there is MONEY Involved, they are normally at the Center of it. (NOTICE that *Wikipedia* only Lists less than 20% of the Owners of Wells Fargo Bank, just to Avoid the Jewish Connections. The Real Owners usually put the Goyim (non-Jews) in Charge of Things, as a False Front, much like the Phony Fronts of Capitalist Stores, which make them Appear to be Good; but, when you Inspect the Backsides of them, you Quickly Discover their Extreme Poverty — Thanks to those Needless Heating and Cooling Bills, Property Taxes, Insurance Bills, and Continual Repairs.)

01-16 [_] O Elected King, I find it most Interesting that Jews are the Owners of most Major Banks, Worldwide, and especially European Banks, where they got a Good Foothold. Therefore, France once Expelled all Jews, after Realizing what a Greedy Selfish Nature they have, which Adolf Hitler also Attempted to do in a more Radical Manner, which ended with the so-called "Holocaust," which is more Rightly called the "HoloHOAX," and for many Reasons that have already been Pointed Out in some of your other Inspired Books, which Reveal that it was another Jewish Exaggeration, much like the Noah's Ark Story in the so-called "Holy Bible," which now has less Credibility than the Holohoax, even though I would Trust the Bible more than Modern-day Fabricators of Outlandish Jewish Lies — such as 4 or 5 Bodies being Stuffed into Nazi Crematory Ovens every 10 Minutes, when any Honest Manager of a Crematorium will freely Confess that it Requires no less than 3 to 4 Hours to Cremate one Adult Body, plus another Hour just to Heat Up the Oven, plus another Hour to Cool it Off before Opening the Door! However, in spite of the Evidence against them, those Lying Red Jews continually Add Numbers to the Alleged Victims of the Holocaust, while Ignoring the FACT that it was American and British Bombs that Destroyed the Railways in Germany, which brought about the Starvation in Prison Camps. Therefore, if anyone is to be Blamed for the Holocaust, it would be the Lying Red Jews who were in Charge of it, which can easily be Proven in a Courtroom. †§‡

01-17 [_] Well, my Friend, there is little Doubt that it was Red Jew Bankers who brought about the Bursting Housing Bubble, which Exposed the Tail of the Snake, you might say; but, not the

Head of the Snake, who is Satan, himself, whose Chief Servants are those Lying Red Jews, which was also True during the Time of Christ, who Orchestrated his Crucifixion and Death: beCause that is their Nature, which is still True until this very Day, who are Chief Weapons Manufacturers for **"The Divided States of United Lies!"** Therefore, there is nothing Secret that shall not be Revealed. ‡ (See *First Corinthians 4:5; Matthew 10:26; Luke 8:17 and 12:2.*)

01-18 [_] O Elected King, I had it in my Mind that the Jews were and still are God's Chosen People, who can do no Wrong. Yes, Blest are those People who Bless the Israelis, who may not be Perfect, like the Palestinians; but, they are Equally as Good. †§‡§§

01-19 [_] Well, you might find it Interesting to Learn that the Palestinians are not Spiritual Cowards, who are not Afraid to Show their Faces at: **"The Great Worldwide TELEVISED Court HEARING,"** while Americans, Brits, and Israelis are TERRIFIED by my Proposals: because the Provable Truths do not make them Look so Good, some of which you can Discover in Howard Zinn's book, called: **"A People's History of the United States."** Yes, it pulls no Punches to their Guts. However, Howard did not get around to making a Thorough Study of the Evil Events of September 11th, 2001, which is the Achilles Heel for those Lying Red Jews, who went a little too Far for their own Good, who brought World Trade Center (WTC) Tower 7 down by Means of Controlled Demolitions in less than 7 Seconds, which could have never been the Case under Natural Conditions: beCause a Hardened Steel Column that is 22-inches by 52-inches by 47 Stories tall, is not going to Collapse into its own Footprint without some POWERFUL Persuasions — such as EXPLOSIVES! Nevertheless, NBC News Reporter, Lester Holt, presented some seemingly "Powerful" Arguments in Favor of the Anti-Christ False Cover-up Federal Government, without Addressing any of the Important Issues that I have Presented — such as HOW such a large Building, which Covered nearly a City Block, could Suddenly Collapse all 283 Hardened Steel Columns in UNISON, like Ballet Dancers hitting the Floor at the Exact same Time, without the Assistance of EXPLOSIVES!? Therefore, it is no Great Wonder WHY more than 3,000 Architects and Engineers just Happen to AGREE with me, after Studying the Case with Reason and Logic, which anyone with an Open Mind can Discover on www.AE911TRUTH.org and other Websites, such as those of Dr. Judy Wood and *Experts Speak Out,* who would have no Interest in making Fools of themselves like the NIST "Scientists," who did not even Inspect the Scenes of the Crimes for Explosives! Some of the Dust has been Saved and Analyzed by Scientists, who say that Explosives were Used. Therefore, the Great Question is, "WHO Installed the Explosives?" Moreover, it Required TIME to get it all Set Up, which was made Possible by the Chief Security Officer, Neil Bush, brother of George Warmonger Bush, and Coconspirator with Larry Silverstein, who Collected about 6 Billion Dollars from those Evil Events: beCause of Collecting Insurance Coverage, who said: "Pull it," when asked what they should Do with WTC Tower 7, which Means to "bring it down," as if he had the Power in his little Finger to Do that without Controlled Demolitions. One of the most Interesting Events during that Day of Woes was the BBC Reporter who told about the Collapse of WTC Tower 7 at least 10 Minutes before it Collapsed, while Standing directly in between it and the Camera that was Recording her! Therefore, one might Rightly Ask, "Just HOW did she Know in Advance that it was going to Collapse?" Moreover, WHO Wrote the Script for her Report, which had to be Written in Advance, which had to be Worded just Exactly Right by some Professional Red Jew, who apparently Forgot to Warn her to Wait until it Actually Collapsed, before giving the Report to the whole World! Therefore, we could call her a Whistleblower, who knew for a Fact that the Report was FALSE: because there is no Way in the World that anyone could have

Known in Advance that such a large Building would Suddenly Decide to Collapse, unless someone was in Control of its Collapse, which they were! Moreover, Lester Holt's Program pointed out that there were several Containers of Fuel Oil that must have EXPLODED within the Tower, before it Collapsed, which likely Caused it to come Down. However, similar Fuel Tanks can be Set Up beside such Large Hardened Steel Columns, right now, in an Experiment to Discover whether or not such Exploding Fuel Tanks can have any Great Effects on all such Steel Columns: beCause, if they could have had any such Drastic Effects, WHY were they Installed within the Building to begin with? Indeed, the New York Fire Department would not have Approved of their Use within the Building, if they were that Dangerous. However, if they did Approve of them, Knowing the Dangers of them, then they should be Charged with Neglect of their Duties, even as the United States Air Force should be Charged with their Neglect to Defend the United States of America from all Enemies, both Foreign and Domestic, and without the Approval of Little Dick Chicanery, even as any Policeman has the Duty to Protect the Citizens from all Enemies, both Foreign and Domestic, which is also True of all of the Armed Forces, who make OATHS of Allegiance to that Affect. Therefore, if a Soldier of any Rank is Riding in an Airplane, and some would-be Terrorist is about to Set Off a BOMB, and that Soldier is Able to Do something to Prevent it, it is his God-given DUTY to Do something about it, with or without the Permission of anyone, just to Keep his OATH of Allegiance! Therefore, what Happened to the Commander of the United States Air Force during September 11th, 2001? Was he Sleeping? Was he Drunk? Was he High on Drugs? Was she having Sex with Chelsea Manning, or what??? Why was he Promoted afterwards for all such Neglect of his Duties? Indeed, the Pentagon is the "Nerve Center" for the entire National Defense Systems, which some Commander FAILED to Protect, who has never been Called to Court for it; but, WHY? †§‡

01-20 [_] O Elected King, I will tell you WHY — it was beCAUSE it was a Federal Government CONSPIRACY for a False Flag Operation! Otherwise, WHY would there be no less than 10 Million Top Secret Documents Locked Up until the Year 4017, concerning that Issue? Indeed, an Innocent Government would Cheerfully Invite any Independent Investigators to Inspect any or all of those Documents, along with the President Kennedy Assassination Documents, which have yet to be Exposed in the Light of Truths in more than 50 Years, as if our National Security might be Endangered by the Fact that VICE-president Lyndon Baines Johnson was in on the Conspiracy with the CIA, FBI, the Mafia, and whomever on Wall Street, who saw it as an Opportunity to Enrich themselves. Even the History Channel came to that same Conclusion, and then Retracted on it. †§‡

01-21 [_] Well, I certainly do not know ALL of the Fine Details; but, many People have Studied such Cases, and have come to the same Conclusion that I have — that all such Documents should be Exposed in the Light of Truths, and Presented to the whole World at: **"The Great Worldwide TELEVISED Court HEARING!"**

— Chapter 02 —

The Chief Criminals Skip Out of Court

02-01 [_] People who Study the Great False Economy are quite Aware of what is going on over there on Wall Street, which has its Financially Rich People, while Billions of People are Suffering in their States of Extreme Poverty. However, as if that were not Bad Enough, those Rich Bankers created the Bursting Housing Bubble, and Caused hundreds of millions of People to Lose Billions of Dollars to them, who were never brought to Court for their Crimes: beCause Rich Red Jew Bankers are Exempt from any Trials for such Crimes: because they have the Power to CRASH the Great False Economy, and would have done so, if American Tax Slaves had not Bailed them Out with nearly a Trillion Dollars, which the Tax Slaves also did for the Automobile Industries, lest they should have also Failed, and thus Americans would have Lost Millions of Jobs, which could have kicked in another Great Depression to have to Deal with, which nobody Wanted. {See www.Amazon.com for: **"The Great False Economy is now DEBUNKED!"** and: **"Are we Tax Slaves of a Lower Order than Lying Red JEWS?" (HOW to be Liberated from all Slavery, Worldwide!) By The Worldwide People's Revolution!®**}

02-02 [_] So, O Elected King, it Sounds as if the Great False Economy is so Fragile that just the Lose of a Million Jobs could CRASH IT; or, a couple of Banks going "Under" could Crash it. However, to "Save" the Great False Economy, and to Prevent another Great Depression, it is Important to Build Up the Production of X-amount of Capitalist Trash to Sell — such as those Junkyard Cars, which hundreds of millions of Ignorant People Depend on for WORK. Otherwise they would be Unemployed: beCause they have no Gardens to Work in, nor any Home-craft Workshops, much less any Well-made Tools to Work with: beCause they have been Deceived by Satan and Sons, Incorporated, who Promote the False Economic System, which is Based on the Silly Notion that Eternal GROWTH is Possible. Therefore, they use Catch Phrases, like: "We must do something to get this Economy Growing again." Indeed, it never Crosses their Weak Minds that if everyone in the World has a Stone Dome Home Complex with Gardens, Cisterns, Home-craft Workshops and Sales Shops, there is no NEED to get the False Economy Growing: because everyone is already Moderately RICH! Therefore, such Rich People have no Need for New Cars nor for any other Capitalist Toys: beCause they are Contented to be Moderately Rich, and even Rejoice for their True Riches, their Security, their Prosperity, their Beautiful Planned City States, their Healthy Happy Children, their Pantries, Coolers, Freezers, and Root Cellars full of Foods, their Churches, Entertainment Centers, Gymnasiums, Swimming Pools, and especially their LUSCIOUS All-Mineral Organic Gardens with Millions of Fruit Trees, Nut Trees, Grape Vines, Berry Bushes, Vegetable Gardens, and Flower Gardens, which they never used to have: beCause of their EXTREME Poverty Under the Rulership of those Lying Red Jew Bankers. ‡

02-03 [_] Well, my Friend, you are Right about all of that, and have Identified the Chief Criminals, who are those People who Promote that Great False Economy, who Ignore the True Economy, which Provides a Way for almost everyone to become Moderately RICH with the Basic Necessities of LIFE, beginning with Fresh Clean Air, Pure Living Water, Good Wholesome Natural Foods, Natural Clothing, Secure Self-air-conditioned Fireproof Tornado-proof Hurricane-proof Rot-proof Paint-proof Termite-proof Mouse-proof Flood-proof Earthquake-proof and Insurance-proof Houses, and Eternal Employment at HOME, or near Home, in their Home-craft Workshops and Sales Shops, where they have Well-made Hand Tools and Machines to Work with, whereby they can make Useful Furniture, Dishes, Clothes, Shoes, Rugs, and even Toys to Play with, as they are Needed and/or Wanted; but, NOT a Billion New Cars that are sitting around in Car Sales Lots waiting for Ignorant Fools to Buy them: so that they can Add their Contaminations to the Air, Water and Land: because no such Vehicles are Needed by Righteous People, who are Contented to be Moderately Rich within their **"Beautiful Swanky PALACES!"** while using Electric Elevators and Subway Trains for Transportation.

02-04 [_] O Elected King, I Hear what you are saying, and it is a Utopian Idea whose Time has now Come; but, there is no Way to Persuade the Masses of People that they should be Contented with the Basic Necessities of Life, when they have been Lusting after the Latest Production of "HOT RODS" — such as those Luxury Cars, which can go 300 Miles per Hour — as if it were Practical to do so, or Necessary for their Happiness, which is nothing but Pride and Vanity! Therefore, these People have a Deep-seated Spiritual Problem, being like Babies who have never Grown Up, who are Pampered by Politicians, who are never Corrected by Preachers, nor by School Teachers, who are Intelligent enough to Know Better, whose Responsibility is to Enlighten the Children's Minds with Provable Truths — such as the Fact that no one on this Earth Needs any such Toys to be Healthy, Wealthy, nor WISE! Indeed, King Solomon and Jesus Christ Lived their entire Lives without any such Toys, and were not Deprived, Depressed, nor Feeling Sorry for themselves, as Spoiled Babies might be, if they do not get their Candies. ‡

02-05 [_] Well, it could be that those Babies are Starving for Natural Fruit Sugars, which are found in Fresh Raw Sweet Fruits — such as Figs, Dates, Grapes, Bananas, Mangos, Cherimoyas, Lychees, Peaches, Pears, Plums, Apricots, Cherries, and Berries. Indeed, such Fruits provide Brain Foods, which are Necessities of LIFE, even as Moses said: beCause the Fruit Trees are the Life of Mankind. (See: *Deuteronomy 20:19, KJV.*) Therefore, if the Children are Craving something Sweet, Feed them some Raisins, Dates, Figs, or some other Sweet Fruits, and some Raw Nuts, whereby they will be Contented and Happy, as well as Energetic. Moreover, if you Feel Tired, you should Sleep, even during the Afternoon, or whenever you get Tired and Sleepy, even as a Baby might do: so that you are also Happy with yourself. Otherwise, you are likely to Overeat, which will Cause you to be Lazy, which will have a Bad Chain-reaction of Things, which may Result with Poverty. ‡

02-06 [_] O Elected King, I had a very Good Thought, just before you made your Statement; but, now I have Lost it: beCause I did not make a Mental Note of it, whereby I might have Remembered it. Indeed, I should have Written it on a Notepad, while it was still in my Mind. So, now it looks like we will never Know what that Great Truth was.

02-07 [_] Well, that has Happened to me many Times, and with Great Regrets, which Truths often come to my Mind during the Night, when I am Trying to Sleep, when I should get Up and Write those Truths on Sticky Notes to Paste on the Bottom of my Computer for Reminders. However, those Sticky Notes would make Distractions from the Flowing Stream of Thoughts that might come to my Mind while Writing a Book: beCause of Wanting to Insert those Sticky Truths into the Book. Therefore, it might be Better to have a Book of Proverbs, whereby all such Random Thoughts can be Collected in the Form of Proverbs. For Example, "O my Son, whenever you Discover a Great Truth, it is Wise of you to Write it in a Book of Proverbs: because it is very likely that other People have also Discovered the same Great Truth, whereby they will be Reminded of it, and thus Enlightened by it." "O my Spiritual Daughter, a Great Truth is one that Applies to all People in all Places, which is Universally True, while a Proverb may not be Universally True; but, only True in certain Circumstances, which is True for most of the Proverbs of King Solomon."

02-08 [_] O Elected King, we need to Meditate on that Great False Economy, which is forever Demanding more and more GROWTH and EXPANSION of Businesses that Produce Various Kinds of Capitalist TRASH for Sale, whereby X-amount of Capitalists have made themselves RICH with the False Riches, while their Work Slaves Barely Survive from Paycheck to Paycheck: beCause they are Attempting to Compete with Cheap Labor Wages in Foreign Countries, which Work Slaves might be Paid as little as 50 Cents per Hour, when they should be getting a Minimum of 20 Dollars per Hour. After all, if those Poor People had lots of Money, they could Afford to Buy those Luxury Cars, and also Afford to Pay Higher Taxes, which Money could be used for Wisely Building WIDER and Longer Interstate Highways for those Countless Cars that might be Sold to them, along with Bumper-to-Bumper Mansions in Remote Places, in Gated Communities, whereby those Middle-class Tax Slaves could Fill their Mansions with Countless Capitalist Products, until the Attics and Basements and Garages are FULL of all such Vain Things, which seldom get Seen, let alone get Used by anyone: beCause all such Junk is simply PILED UP, until those Spaces are FILLED; and then it is Time for a Yard Sale, whereby X-amount of Ignorant People can wander by and Discover something to Stuff into their Attics, Basements, or Garages. Otherwise, they can Rent Storage Boxes around Town, whereby they can Fill them with that Junk, whereby they can be Happy, knowing that the Angels of Heaven are Smiling down on them for Neglecting the Needs of the Billions of Extremely Poor People in this World of Woes, who do not even have Gardens to Feed themselves, much less Reliable Cisterns for Water Storage for those Gardens, as well as Water Pumps and Electricity to Run them: because they Live in Mud Huts and Bamboo Shanties, in Slums and Ghettos, in the most Deplorable Conditions, and all for the LACK of **"The New RIGHTEOUS One-World Government!"** †§‡§§

02-09 [_] So, my Friend, are you Suggesting that all of those Big Babies need someone in Charge of them, to Properly Manage them, to Control their Money, or what??

02-10 [_] Well, O Elected King, with a RIGHTEOUS Government, the Masses of Young People would be HIRED to Build their own **"Beautiful Swanky PALACES,"** whereby there would be no Desire to Stuff their Garages with Capitalist TRASH: beCause they would have Beautiful Places to Live and Work, who would mostly be Working at Home, or near Home, and only for 3 to 4 Hours per Day, which would give to them Plenty of Time to Study the Good Books, and to Play Musical Instruments, and to Visit other Beautiful Swanky Palaces in other **"GLORIOUS Swanky Hotels Castles and Fortresses,"** which would be Marvelous Places with all of their Palaces with their Gardens, Vineyards, and Orchards. Yes, there would be Special Workshops for Special Arts and Crafts, which would be most Fascinating; but, not so Fascinating as your Marvelous Literature, which tells about other Worlds and Strange People, including the Giants, UFO's, Aliens, and the Insides of other Planets.

(It is Time for some Sane Person to get Control of this Insane World!)

— Chapter 03 —

The Perfect Economic System

03-01 [_] The Perfect Economic System would have to be Good for ALL Peoples, Worldwide, and not just Good for Rich Hogs on Wall Street and similar Places around the World, whereby Rich People have taken Advantage of the Poor People, and made them into their SLAVES. Indeed, it is a Typical Red Jew Plan to make Slaves of other People, even while Proclaiming Freedom, Liberty, and Justice for ALL!

03-02 [_] O Elected King, it seems to me that you are Proposing to make almost everyone on the Earth into a SLAVE, yourself, just to Build those **"GLORIOUS Swanky Hotels Castles and Fortresses,"** which will Require no less than 20 Years of Slavery, just to get them BUILT, even with the Assistance of those Mechanical Slaves — such as Bulldozers, Backhoes, Track-hoes, Cranes, Front-end Loaders, Forklifts, Electric Trains, Rock-cutting Machines, Rock-polishing Machines, Concrete Mixers, and all of the Useful Tools that you have Proposed: beCause there will be TRILLIONS of Tiles to be Set on Stone Walls, even within those Swanky Cisterns. †§‡

03-03 [_] Well, it is True that there will be LOTS of Work for everyone to Do, until those Swanky Fortresses are Finished, about a thousand Years from now; but, after they are Finished, Life will be rather Easy. Moreover, if anyone is not Willing nor Able to Learn and Work, they are Welcome to Live in some Old Rusty Used Van, down by the Riverside with BIG Fat Farley, Huck Finn and Nigger Jim: because it will not Bother me the Slightest Bit if they Starve to Death! After all, there are some People who are Beyond Redemption without the Assistance of Sicknesses, Diseases, Accidents, Famines, Wars, Plagues, Earthquakes, Tornadoes, Hurricanes, Fires, Floods, Mudslides and other Spooky Events, which seem to Wake them Up — at least for a certain Period of Time, after which they normally have Relapses, and Slip Back into the same Dirty Greasy Pits that they used to be in. However, with the Economic System that I Propose, almost all People will become Gardeners, whereby they will Maintain Balanced Minds to some Degree, being Closer to Nature and Nature's God, and former President Thomas Jefferson might say. However, since most People do not Like Gardening: beCause of not being Bonded to it, they may Choose to let **"The Swanky Association of Professional Gardeners"** do their Gardening for them, while they Join **"The Swanky Association of House Cleaners,"** or **"The Swanky Associations of Professional Cooks,"** or some other Swanky Association of Working Soldiers, whereby they can do an Average of 4 Hours of Common Unskilled Labor per Day, 6 Days per Week, or the Equivalent thereof, and thus have a Fine Living. In Fact, that is also what I would Choose to Do, if I were a Young Man: because I would Understand that if I Joined **"The Swanky Associations of Working Soldiers,"** all of my Needs and Wants would be Fulfilled. Indeed, my Foods, Drinks, Clothing, Tools, Water, Garden, Transportation, Electricity, TV, and everything would be FREE, in Exchange for Doing whatever I might be Asked to Do for 4 Hours per Day. Moreover, if I Wanted more Money to Buy something, I would be Free to do more Work for Good Swanky Wages. ‡ {See: **"A List of FAIR Swanky Wages!" (The Equitable Wage System!) By The Worldwide People's Revolution!® Book 065.**}

03-04 [_] O Elected King, after those Swanky Fortresses are Finished, it might be Possible for everyone to do as little as 2 Hours of Work per Day, just to Feed and Clothe themselves; but, I would Prefer to Work for 8 Hours per Day, whereby I might Accumulate some Silver or Gold: because I Like those Heavy Metals, which give to me a Sense of False Pride, you might say, even though it is Wise to have some Money for Retirement. After all, no Government can be Trusted that far into the Future: because our Elected King might be Dead, and a Wicked King might Arise, who will make all of us Revert Back into Tax Slaves for his own Gain. †§‡

03-05 [_] Well, I Seriously Doubt that any Wicked King will Arise, if all Elected Officials must Fill Out and File **"The Complete SURVEYS of our VALUES,"** before being Elected, which everyone will be Welcome to Study. However, even if it were Possible, there would be no Possibility of any such Person Conquering Millions of those **"GLORIOUS Swanky Hotels Castles and Fortresses!" (Beautiful Planned City States for WISE Intelligent Well-Educated People with Common Sense and Good Understanding!):** beCause all such Fortresses would be Built for SELF-DEFENSE! Therefore, if **"The New RIGHTEOUS One-World Government"** has Limited Powers, according to: **"The CONSTITUTION for the New RIGHTEOUS One-World GovernMint,"** what are the Chances of anyone being made into a SLAVE for some Wicked King? Answer: ZILCH!

03-06 [_] O Elected King, if the Present Evil Empire has its Way, almost everyone in the World will be Branded with the Mark of the Beast, whereby they will not be Able to Buy nor Sell anything without their RFID Chip, whereby their Present Established Governments will have Total Control over the Masses of People, which is what they have always Wanted — NOT their True Prosperity, whereby the Masses of People might have Total Control over themselves, and not Live in Fear of any Wicked Governments! ‡

03-07 [_] Well, if the Masses of People were WISE, they would do their Best to Elect ME to be their RIGHTEOUS King, whereby we could Guarantee them to be Secure within their Swanky Fortresses, and to be Free from any Monster Governments. After all, it is Possible for a Small Swanky Fortress to be Self-sufficient and Independent from all of the others, if there is only 10,000 Skilled People among them, who could also Trade with Similar Swanky Fortresses by Means of Underground Subway Trains; and thus not Live in Fear of any Invaders. However, for what Reason would anyone be Interested in Invading other Cities? Has Los Angeles ever Attacked Chicago, New York City, or Houston, Texas? Of course not: beCause the Federal Government would not Allow it to Happen. Likewise, **"The New RIGHTEOUS One-World Government"** would not Allow any Nation to Attack any other Nation; but, it would Assist all Nations to Build their own **"GLORIOUS Swanky Hotels Castles and Fortresses!"** Therefore, once they get Built, the Devil and his Demon Spirits will be Bound in Shackles and Chains, you might say; and thus that will be End of Confusion! {See www.Amazon.com for: **"The END of CONFUSION!" (The Great CELEBRATION of the Magnificent Wedding of the Humble Honest Nations, and the Grand Year of JUBILEE!) By The Worldwide People's Revolution!® Book 050.**}

03-08 [_] O Elected King, we can hardly Wait for that Glorious Day, which was not Possible before Modern Means of Communications, whereby the Masses of People might Tweet their Messages, such as: "The GWTCH, April 21," which will be a Signal for all Believers to Stay at Home and Stay in BED: beCause of being SICK of the Great False Economy, whereby the

Leaders of all Nations will be FORCED to Attend: **"The Great Worldwide TELEVISED Court HEARING!" (That Great Meeting of the Most Intelligent Minds!) By The Worldwide People's Revolution!**® Book 041. Yes, they will either Cooperate and Attend that Meeting, or else their Great False Economy will CRASH: beCause the Masses of People will Refuse to Buy anything, which will be a Peaceful Bloodless REVOLUTION! Therefore, the Military Industrial Congressional Bankers' Complex will have to SUBMIT to Reason and Logic! Otherwise, when those Protestors go Back to Work, it will be to make WAR against them, and BURN DOWN all of those Ugly Cities of Confusion, and LOOT and PLUNDER all of the Stores, and make the Watts Fires look like a Sunday Picnic! (See *Wikipedia* for *Watts Riots*.) †§‡

03-09 [_] Well, if the Masses of People are PATIENT, there will be NO Wars, nor Riots, much less any Cities being Burned. However, knowing the Nature of most People, it is Doubtful that they will OBEY their Elected King, and Stay at Home and FAST and PRAY, even as I have Asked them to Do, come next April 21st: beCause that is a Good Time to Fast, while the Gardens are Growing, whereby they might have something to Eat after Fasting, and especially Fresh Greens, which are Laxative and Good for SWEEPING OUT their Bowels after Fasting. I Prefer Kale Greens, which should be Steamed until they are Tender, which can be Seasoned with some Olive Oil, or even some Dressing, and Eaten with Green Raw Onions and Steamed Red Garden Beets, which are very Laxative, which can be Planted just as soon as the Garden Soil can be Worked during the Springtime, which will Require about 60 Days to Mature. Therefore, the Timing is Important, or else the Fasting may Prove to be Detrimental, instead of Beneficial. Nevertheless, the Objective is to Persuade the Leaders of all Nations to Attend: **"The Great Worldwide TELEVISED Court HEARING,"** whereby I might Ask them a few Important Questions, which are Outlined within that Inspired Book, and also in other Inspired Books.

03-10 [_] So, O Elected King, if Worse Conditions comes to the WORST Conditions, all of those Cities of Confusion will be Destroyed, come next Summer, and then the Governments of the World will be Dethroned, and all of the Politicians will be Hanged, and the Bankers will be Crucified and Roasted in Nazi Ovens, and the Lawyers will be Stripped, Tarred and Feathered, and Rode Out of Town on Spiked Rails, along with all Judges, Medical Doctors, Professors, and Preachers, unless they Join **The Worldwide People's Revolution!**® Therefore, that could Prove to be the Undoing of the Evil Empire, which would be very PAINFUL to Endure, as Opposed to Submitting to: **"The Swanky Sword of Divine Truths,"** which only Asks for a FAIR Hearing at: **"The Great Worldwide TELEVISED Court HEARING!"** Yes, it might Prove to be Embare-assing for those Rich Hogs and Lying Red Jews; but, if they Confess their Wrongdoings, they will Live through it, and end up Living within their own **"Beautiful Swanky PALACES!"**

— Chapter 04 —

WHO Qualifies to be the Elected King?

04-01 [_] Well, if you are Looking for a RIGHTEOUS Person to Elect, you need not Look any farther than the Inspired Author of more than 350 Good Books, including this one, which may be Offensive to certain Lying Red Jews, or Edomites; but, that is only beCause they have not Confessed all of their Sins, beginning with their GREED, who can also be Forgiven, IF they Ask for Forgiveness. However, they would first of all have to Discover just how GREEDY and SELFISH they are, who should have to Sleep under some Freeway Bridges, and in Subway Sewage Systems, just to be Able to Relate with the Billions of Poor People in this World of Woes, who may not be Living under Freeway Bridges, nor in Subway Sewage Systems; but, it is for Sure that they are not Eating at Royal Swanky Buffets, nor Living in Million-dollar Mansions with all of the Luxuries that are Enjoyed by those Rich HOGS, who Look Down on them as Rats and Snakes, when they, themselves, are Worse than Rats and Snakes, who are without any Empathy at all, whose Consciences are DEAD, if they do not Wholeheartedly Agree with ME — that it is now Time to Establish **"The New RIGHTEOUS One-World Government!" (HOW to Establish a Righteous One-World Government without Going to WAR!) By The Worldwide People's Revolution!® Book 056.**

04-02 [_] O Elected King, it would Require HONESTY for them to Confess that they have been Greedy Selfish HOGS. However, I have Heard that you also Live in a Marble Palace, in a Million-dollar House with no less than 6,000 square feet of Space — as if you Needed such a House, when you could be Living in a Mud Hut, or Adobe Shanty with Scorpions Waltzing about all Night, whereby you might also be Able to Relate with those Billions of Poor People. †§

04-03 [ ] Well, in spite of Living in a Million-dollar House, it does not Belong to me, even as the White House in Washington does not Belong to the President; but, he gets to Live in it. Indeed, I Sold almost all of my Possessions, just to Build the House that I Live in, which was only made Possible by the Cooperation of a Mexican Family, who Helped me and my Brother Vern to Build it. Otherwise, none of us would have any Houses to Live in, except for perhaps one of those Adobe Huts that you were referring to, which used to be Standard Normal Houses in Mexico: because they did not have Concrete to Work with, Years Ago, much less the Money to Buy it, even though they were plenty Willing to do the Work. After all, it has been Reported that Mexicans are the Hardest Working People in the World, which you could Discover by Trading Jobs with them. For Example, Try Picking 4,000 Pounds of Tomatoes in a Hot Field in Florida, each Day, for a Month, while Bending Over, and only get 40$ for doing it.

04-04 [_] So, O Elected King, it seems that the Hebrew God is NOT on your Side, or else you would be Blest with Great Riches, like Bill Computer Software Gates, who Built a 50-million-dollar Mansion for himself, in Washington State, who does not even Live in it for most of the Time: beCause of his Missionary Work in Africa, India, Bangladesh, Pakistan, China, and wherever, huh? Indeed, God should have Blest you with enough Money to Mail a Copy of this Book to every Mailbox in **"The Divided States of United Lies!" (The so-called "United States**

(It is Time for some Sane Person to get Control of this Insane World!)

of North America" in Disguise!) Book 058. However, if God Sincerely Wanted you to be his Selected King for **"The New RIGHTEOUS One-World Government,"** he would have Provided a Way for you to take over the Whole World without Firing a Shot! {See: **"The United States of the Whole World!" (A True Global Economy for the Masses of Working People!) By The Worldwide People's Revolution!®** Book 055.}

04-05 [_] Well, God is not Interested in FORCING People to Live Righteous Lives, nor to Establish a Righteous One-World Government: beCause it is his Will that People should Learn the Truths that can Liberate them from their Prisons of Lies, and make it Possible for them to be Free in all Ways, beginning with Freedom from their Sins, which are Transgressions of his Divine Laws. Therefore, after People have Suffered Long Enough, they will come to their Riit Senses, and thus Change their Minds, even as the Prodigal Son of *Luke 15* Changed his Mind, and Decided to Return to his Father, and Volunteer to be an Obedient Servant, which all of us should now Decide to Do, becoming Servants of one another, just as the Apostle Peter Suggested, who was Far Ahead of his Time. (See *First Peter 5:5—11, KJV*.)

04-06 [_] O Elected King, I do not Object to Submitting to a RIGHTEOUS King, nor even to a Righteous Employer: because a Righteous Person would not be Asking me to Say nor Do any Evil Thing. However, I do Object to Submitting to a WICKED ANTI-CHRIST FALSE COVER-UP TAX-MASTER Federal Government, which Wastes my Tax Money on Vain Things that are not Needed, nor Wanted by Righteous People. For Example, they Wasted no less than 16 Trillion Dollars on the War Games in the Middle East, including the "Eternal" Support of Veterans, or Victims of Capitalism, who will have to be Supported by us Tax Slaves until they Die! Indeed, if that same Amount of Money had been Spent WISELY, all of the People in the Middle East could have now been Living in those **"Beautiful Swanky PALACES!" (A New Concept in Living Habits — Swanky Palaces for Poor People!) By The Worldwide People's Revolution!®** Book 066.

04-07 [_] Well, most of those Poor People would have Gladly Volunteered to Help Build their own Swanky Palaces, if only they had been Provided with the Necessary Well-made Tools to Work with, which would have Cost far less than those Extremely Expensive War Machines. For Example, a large Bulldozer is less than one-tenth the Price of an Army Tank, and not one-hundredth the Price of a Jet Bomber, which must have Precise Parts with no Space for any Errors, while a Bulldozer does not have to be Perfect, just as long as it is Workable. However, in most Cases, those Poor People only needed some Materials to Work with, which they could Trade their Labor for, if they had Righteous Governments. Nevertheless, the Way that God Arranged this World, the Natural Resources are all Scattered Out around the World, which Requires Worldwide Cooperation, in Order to Truly Prosper. For Example, most of the Zinc and Diamonds come from South Africa, while most of the Rocks can only be found in the Great Mountain Ranges, not on the Great Plains, nor on the Great Savannas.

04-08 [_] So, O Elected King, do you Sincerely Believe that YOU Qualify to be the Elected King of **"The New RIGHTEOUS One-World Government"**? Do you even have a Grade School Education?

04-09 [_] Well, I would say that I have far more Education than King Solomon, and he seemed to do Well: beCause he had what is called WISDOM, even though one would Wonder about that, considering how many Silly Wives he had, who must have been Extremely Depressed for a Lack of Attention! Indeed, just Exactly HOW could any Man Satisfy even 10 Women, let alone 1,000 of them, seeing that just one Woman can "Service" a hundred Men, Sexually? In Fact, Notorious Prostitutes have done it on a Regular Basis during Wartimes, when Soldiers have Lined Up by the hundreds, just to Relieve themselves, which I have Witnessed with my own Eyeballs, which I found very Repulsive and Disgusting, even as the Prostitutes also no doubt found it, who must have been Sick of it within a Week or less. Nevertheless, for the Love of Money, People will Say and Do just about anything, which was probably the Case with King Solomon, who had LOTS of Money to Waste on his Women. However, my Qualifications Depend on my most Reasonable Solutions for our Massive Problems, which no one else has to Offer. Otherwise, they might Challenge me with their Dull Rubber swords. {See: **"The Swanky Sword of Divine Truths!"**}

04-10 [_] So, O Elected King, do you not have any Practical Experience with Leadership, at all? Have you never been Elected for any Political Office, nor even Managed a Business?

04-11 [_] Well, I have Managed a few Working Soldiers on Construction Jobs; but, I never did have Enough Money to Work with, whereby we might have done something Correctly. Therefore, it follows the Proverb of King Solomon, *"The Rich Man's Wealth is his Strong City; but, the Destruction of the Poor People is their Poverty." — Proverbs 10:15.*

04-12 [_] So, a Righteous Government would make Sure that everyone had an Abundance of Money to Work with, huh? But, what about Wasting Money on Vain Projects — such as Greenhouses in Alaska for Fruit Trees, or Airplane Runways in the Sahara Desert in Africa?

04-13 [_] Well, a Righteous King would do his Best to be Conservative, and not Waste any Time, Materials, Energy, nor Money on Vain Projects, nor on Worthless Politicians, Lawyers, Medical Doctors, Professors, nor even Fire DEPARTments: beCause of Building those **"GLORIOUS Swanky Hotels Castles and Fortresses!" (Beautiful Planned City States for WISE Intelligent Well-Educated People with Common Sense and Good Understanding!) By The Worldwide People's Revolution!® Book 019.** Indeed, the School Teachers can give their Classes on Special TV Channels, for Free, if they have anything Important to Teach. Likewise, the Preachers can Preach their Sermons on Special TV Channels, after we Prove whatever is Worthy to be Preached: beCause we have Heard enough Lies. Therefore, a Righteous King would Challenge their False Doctrines, and make them Defend their Beliefs, beginning with that Religious Nonsense about People going to Heaven when they Die, when everyone with a Right Mind Knows for a Fact that they all go down to their Graves, if they are not Cremated, or Blasted Away with Bombs, Rockets, Mortars, Grenades, Mines, and other Hateful Weapons, which Sane People would get RID of. However, if anyone Disagrees, and Wants to Keep all such Weapons, his House should be made into an Ammunition Dump, even as Rich Bankers should have Hot Molten Gold poured down their Throats, if they cannot Explain to us WHY it is a Good Reason to Stockpile thousands of Tons of Gold in their Bank Vaults, which should be used Wisely for Decorating Churches, Mosques, Synagogues, Temples, Theaters, Auditoriums, Concert Halls, and **"Beautiful Swanky PALACES!"** †§‡

04-14 [_] So, O Elected King, would you Rob all of the Rich Bankers, who have Stockpiles of Gold in their Banks? Would you Steal it from them, or what?? What would Jesus do with all such Gold Reserves?

(It is Time for some Sane Person to get Control of this Insane World!)

04-15 [_] Well, some People would say that almost all Gold and Silver should be used for Minting Coins, or making MONEY, which People should have to Earn by Honest Labor, which is not a Bad Idea, except that it Automatically Invites Thieves and Robbers to Arise from the Woodwork, you might say, which is BAD: beCause it is much Better to not have any Money at all, nor to Set any Monetary Value on anything: beCause it only Leads to Corruption. For Example, we should have Swanky Tool Houses within all Swanky Fortresses, which have Plenty of Tools to Work with, which everyone should be able to Help themselves to, just as long as they take Good Care of those Tools. Otherwise, they should Return those Tools to the Tool Houses, if they are not Using them, whereby other People might Use them, even as I have already Explained in another Book. However, if someone Wants to Earn the necessary "Credits" to "Buy" such Tools, they would be Welcome to do that, which Tools might even be of Superior Quality than those Tools in the Tool Houses, all of which must be Graded for their Qualities. Nevertheless, I would not Want any Silver nor Gold made into Money: because it might get Lost, Stolen, Robbed, or otherwise just Wear Out; but, I would use it Wisely for everyone to Enjoy its Beauty, and not Hide it in any Bank Vaults. Moreover, if those Rich Bankers do not Cooperate to Do that, they should Present their Arguments at: **"The Great Worldwide TELEVISED Court HEARING,"** whereby we might come to Understand their Objections. Likewise, if anyone has a Legitimate Objection to anything that I Propose, he or she should Present his or her Objections at that Great Meeting of the Most Intelligent Minds, whereby we might Agree with such Arguments, and even Vote concerning them. ‡ {See the Cover Photo for: **"WHY are some Preachers so POOR?" (HOW almost all Preachers could get Moderately RICH, without Preaching any Outlandish LIES!) By The Worldwide People's Revolution!® Book 009.**}

04-16 [_] O Elected King, I just Happen to Like DOGS. Therefore, will I be Able to Keep my Dogs, when we Build those **"GLORIOUS Swanky Hotels Castles and Fortresses!"**?

04-17 [_] Well, you only have to Check the above Box [_] with an X, as well as the Previous Boxes in this Verse, which will let the Computers know that you Want to Live with People who Like Dogs.

    A-[_] I Like Anteaters and Alligators, and Want to Live with them.

    B-[_] I Like Bats, Bees, and Bookworms, and Want to Live with them.

    C-[_] I Like House Cats, Cockroaches, and Criminals, and Want to Live with them.

    D-[_] I Like Donkeys, Ducks, and Dingbats, and Want to Live with them.

    E-[_] I Like Elephants, Eels, and E-mail Letters, and Want to Live with them.

    F-[_] I Like Ferrets, Factories, and Fads, and Want to Live with them.

    G-[_] I Like God, Good Governments, and Galaxies, and Want to Live with him.

    H-[_] I Like Hermits, Horses, and Hunters, and Want to Live with them.

    I-[_] I Like Insane People, and Want to Live with them.

J-[_] I Love Jesus, and Want to Live with him; but, not Sleep with him. §

K-[_] King Jesus will not Sleep with anyone: because he Loves everyone. †§‡§§

L-[_] I Like Llamas, Alpacas, Vicunas, and Guanacos, and Want to Live with them.

M-[_] I Like Monkeys, Moon-rovers, and Macadamias, and Want to Live with them.

N-[_] I Like Nocturnal Creatures, such as Screech Owls, who have 3 Eyelids — one for the Daytime Hunting, one for the Nighttime Hunting, and one for Sleeping. Indeed, all 3 Eyelids are Closed for Sleeping, while 2 Inner Eyelids are used for Daytime Hunting, and one is use for Nighttime Hunting, just to Protect the Eyes from Insects, Leaves, Twigs, and Dust. †

O-[_] I Like Owls of all Kinds, Ocelots, Octopuses, and Ostriches, and Want to Live with them.

P-[_] I Like Penguins, Pelicans, Parrots, Pheasants, and Peacocks, and Want to Live with them. (You may ~~Cross Out~~ any that you do not Like.)

Q-[_] I Like Queers, and Want to Live with them: beCause I am a Queen, myself, which is Questionable. §

R-[_] I Like Robbins, Robots, Rubies, and Rubble, and Want to Live with them.

S-[_] I Like Snakes, Snails, Slugs, Sloths, Sea Gulls, and Sea Shells, and Want to Live with them.

T-[_] I Like Turtles, Terrapins, Termites, Teetsee Flies, and Tortoises, and Want to Live with them.

U-[_] I Understand that I can Live with any Animals that I Like; but, I cannot make Prisoners of any of them: because I would not Want to be made into a Prisoner, myself.

    U2-[_] I Want to Live in a Swanky Fortress that has a Natural Zoo.

V-[_] I Like Vampire Bats, Various Varmints, and Vermin, and Want to Live with them in a Damp Musty Cave.

W-[_] I Like Woolly Mammoth Elephants, Wolverines, and Wolves, and Want to Live with them.

X-[_] X-amount of People Love Horses; but, that does not Mean that they Want to Live in Barns with them and their Cows. [_] I Want a Horse to Love.

Y-[_] I Like Yaks, Bisons, Water Buffalos, Musk Oxens, Reindeers, Elks, Caribous, and Mooses, and Want to Live with them.

Z-[_] I Like Zebras, and Want to Live with them, who are sometimes called Mulattos.

04-18 [_] O Elected King, are you Willing to Debate any Challengers, if they should arise among us?

04-19 [_] Of course! Please Step Up and Present yourself at: **"The Great Worldwide TELEVISED Court HEARING,"** if only to Protest Against **"The New RIGHTEOUS One-World Government,"** since your Questions can be Answered, and your Disputations Solved. Better yet, why not Present your Arguments in: **"FREEDUM uv SPEECH!" (U Speshoul Maguzeen uv Onust Upinyunz!) By The Worldwide People's Revolution!®** Book 030.

04-20 [_] O Elected King, I can hardly wait to Learn just HOW you would Deal with Abortions in your Righteous Kingdom.

04-21 [_] Well, I cannot Remember just which one of my Multitude of Books Addresses that Subject; but, it is Possible to Discover it, and every Sane Person will Agree with it.

04-22 [_] So, O King, are you saying that if someone Disagrees with you, that he or she is Insane?

04-23 [_] NO! They be they might be only be Ignorant. Therefore, if they Disagree with me, they should Educate themselves, or else Educate me: because I am Happy to Change my Mind about any Subject, which is one of those Good Things that Qualifies me to be your Elected King! †§‡

04-24 [_] I do not Trust a Person who Changes his or her Mind about any Subject. For Example, God Wanted to Destroy all of the Israelites for their Sins; but, Moses Argued Against it, and God Changed his Mind. Therefore, I do not Trust God. †§‡§§ (See *Exodus 32 and Deuteronomy 9*.)

04-25 [_] O Selected King, if you do not Change your Mind about Aborting Babies, I will not Vote for you to be our Elected King.

04-26 [_] And have you Studied my Beliefs concerning Abortions?

04-27 [_] No; but, I have Heard that you are Pro-abortions, Pro-Animal Riits, and Pro-LGBTQs.

04-28 [_] Well, there are 3 Options to Choose from, and I have Chosen the Third Option, which you have Obviously NOT Studied. Therefore, do not Listen to any False Rumors.

04-29 [_] O King, a Person either Believes in Aborting Babies, or does not Believe in it. There are no other Options: beCause a Baby is a New Person just as soon as he or she is Conceived in the Womb. Therefore, it is Wrong to Murder any Baby of any Size. ‡

04-30 [_] Well, that is no doubt your Honest Opinion; but, there is a Third Option, which is Biblical and most Practical, for which you cannot Present any Reasonable Argument: because it is a Commandment of GOD!

— Chapter 05 —

Would a Righteous King Force his Subjects to Believe as he Believes?

05-01 [_] The Short Answer is, NO, Absolutely NOT! However, he would Naturally do his Best to Enlighten as many Minds as Possible with his Inspired Words of Provable Truths.

05-02 [_] So, O Elected King, how come you did not take up a few Pages in this Book to Explain to us what you Believe about Abortions, whereby our Minds might be Enlightened?

05-03 [_] Well, why should I *Rewrite* a Chapter that can already be "red" by whomever is Interested in that Subject? Indeed, that would be a Waste of Time, Materials, Energy, and Money: beCause I Plan on making a Master Index to all of my Inspired Books during the Future, whereby you will easily be Able to Discover such Subjects, and especially if those Subjects are Rarely Mentioned — such as Abortions, Gun Violence, Suicides, and Presidential Debates. †§‡

05-04 [_] O Elected King, I will be "Forever" Tormented, until I Learn what your Belief is about Abortions: beCause that could be your Achilles Heel in Politics, if you know what I Mean.

05-05 [_] Trust me, I am NOT a Potential Tyrant King: beCause it is my Belief that each Person may have his or her own Beliefs, and Live with other People of Like-mindedness within the Swanky Fortresses of their Choices, which is one of the most Beautiful Things about my Master Plan: because it Provides True Freedom for everyone to Practice their Religious and Political Beliefs, just as long as they do NOT Believe some of those Radical Teachings in the "Uninspired" Writings of Moses — such as *Deuteronomy 7*, which Demands the Children of Israel to Slaughter ALL of the Hittites, Girgashites, Amorites, Canaanites, Perizzites, Hivites, Jebuzites, and whomever was in the "Promised Land," which was taken from them by FORCE of Arms, which was a Satanic Act, in my Honest Opinion: beCause Jesus said that if the same Miracles had been done in Sodom and Gomorra, which he did in Capernaum, those Sodomites would have Repented in Sackcloth while sitting in Ashes, which would have been a Compassionate Way to Save them by getting them Converted, rather than by Murdering them, whereby the Israelites Disobeyed the Commandment of God to not Murder. Therefore, which one of the following Boxes will you Check with an X?

    A-[_] I Agree with the Commandment of God to not Murder. They should have Obeyed.

    B-[_] I Believe that the Contradictory Hebrew God was Insane for Asking Innocent Young Men to Murder those Canaanites, whereby they would be Guilt-ridden for the Remainder of their Lives for Dashing the Heads of the Babies against Stone Walls, or even running Swords through their Hearts.

    C-[_] I Confess that I am Greatly Confused by the Commandments of God.

(It is Time for some Sane Person to get Control of this Insane World!)

D-[_] DUMBmocracy should have Voted on it, rather than Obey some Insane God, who Forgot about his own Dignity, whom no Righteous Person could Honor: beCause Murder is Murder, no matter HOW one goes about Doing it, with or without the Permission of some Unknown God.

E-[_] Educated People would have made Boats, and then Travelled to some Unoccupied Land, to Inherit it, and thus left those Canaanites alone.

F-[_] I Fail to Understand what was WRong with Killing 6 million or so Canaanites, who had become Fully Ripe in their Iniquities, saith the Irreverent LOUDMOUTH Slothgut Windbag Hole-in-Thy-Head!

G-[_] God knows that it was a Test of the Faith of the Israelites in his Commandments.

H-[_] HUMBUG! Which Commandments were they supposed to have Faith in — the one that said to not Murder, or the one that said to Murder Innocent Children and Kid Goats?

I-[_] I See what you Mean — they should have only Murdered half of them, and then they would have been Obeying both Commandments at the same Time. †§‡

J-[_] Justice Demands that they should have Killed only the Guilty ones, and left the Innocent ones Alive, including their Snakes and Scorpions.

K-[_] King Jesus would not have Killed any of them: because the *Scriptures* say, *"Dearly Beloved, Avenge not yourselves; but, rather give a Place for the Wrath of God: because it is written, Vengeance is mine, I will Repay, says the Supreme Ruler." — Romans 12:19.* Therefore, God should have gotten his Wrath on them by Means of some Plague, just like he got Rid of the American Indians, who were Smoking too many Peace Pipes. †§‡§§

L-[_] Lots of Laughs! King Jesus will Return as *"the Lion of the Tribe of Judah,"* who will Destroy all of his Enemies. †§ (See *Revelation 5:5* and *Zechariah 12:9.*)

M-[_] It is not Morally Correct to take any Words Out of Context, even if the Apostle Paul did it Regularly, who got the Idea from *Matthew 2,* which has no Connection with the Actual Birth of Jesus Christ.

N-[_] Not everyone is Interested in any such Religious Nonsense. I would like to Hear a Debate between our Elected King and the Presidential Candidates. (See the next Chapter.)

O-[_] I am Opposed to all Political Debates: because True Christians do not get themselves Entangled in all such Spider Webs.

P-[_] People in general Love Good Debates, just as long as their Opponents are not Winning.

Q-[_] The Great Question is this: **"Will those Political Spiritual COWARDS ever be Willing to Confront our Elected King with their Dull Rubber Swords, which cannot even Stand Up on their own?"** Chances are that they will not.

R-[_] Rightly or wRongly, our Elected King will easily Defeat his Enemies when they Appear at: **"The Great Worldwide TELEVISED Court HEARING!" (That Great Meeting of the Most Intelligent Minds!) By The Worldwide People's Revolution!®**

S-[_] Satan was also Good with his Arguments with Christ; but, he Lost, and Christ Won. (See *Matthew 4*.)

T-[_] Satan did not Understand just HOW to Tempt Christ: so that he might have Won. Indeed, after Jesus Fasted for 40 Days and 40 Nights, Satan should have Tempted him with a Gallon of Fresh Fragrant Coconut Water / Mango / Papaya Smoothie with Strawberries and Blueberries in a Side Dish, which some Unholy Angel could have Delivered to him in the Name of Jehovah God. †§

U-[_] The Ultimate Temptation at that Time would have been a Gallon of Immature Coconut Water with the Juice of a couple of Ripe Limes; but, Satan was not a Good Cook. †§

V-[_] The Victory will be to him who Resists all *Evil* Temptations, *not* Good ones. For Example, if you are 20 Years Old, and a really Beautiful Woman Wants to Marry you, it is Better to Yield to that Temptation, rather than go Looking for some Ugly Painted Skunk, who does not even Love you, who only Wants your Money. †§‡

W-[_] And what makes you Imagine that such a Woman will Actually Love you half as much as that Ugly Painted Skunk, seeing that she only Wants your Money? †§

X-[_] X-amount of Ignorant People like to Gamble with their Lives, and Marry just whomever Happens to come along, as if they were Sent by God for Better or for Worse, rather than being Wise, and Demanding that all such Lovers should Fill Out and File **"The Complete SURVEYS of our VALUES!"** — whereby they might have some Idea what that Potential Life-mate might Believe, whereby they might Discover some Compatible Person to Live with, rather than Gamble on it. After all, if they have nothing in Common, except Sex, how Happy is that Marriage going to be?

Y-[_] I would be Wise and Yield to the First Woman who is Brave enough to Grab my Crotch, even if she had Leprosy. †§‡§§

Z-[_] You must be a Republican Zebra with very Short Ears.

05-06 [_] I Believe that it is the Duty of all Elected Kings to Preach the Truths that they Believe, even if all of those so-called "Truths" can be Proven to be WRong. †§‡

05-07 [_] I Believe that Religion has no Place in the Government: because Moral Values have nothing to do with Right Decisions. †§‡

05-08 [_] I Believe that the Pope of Rome or the Rev. Billy Graham would make Better Leaders than Politicians: because they would at least Practice some of the Teachings of Jesus Christ.

(It is Time for some Sane Person to get Control of this Insane World!)

05-09 [_] I am Sick of all of them, with or without their Phony Religions.

05-10 [_] I Want to Hear that Great Debate between our Elected King and American Candidates for the Presidency.

— Chapter 06 —

Our Elected King Debates the Presidential Candidates

06-01 [_] It would be Nice if this Chapter were Timeless, whereby it might Apply to all Election Deceptions of Dimwitcrats and Reprobates, who have been Voting for the Rong/Riit Right/WRong Parties for more than 200 Years, while Servicing Rich Bankers with Trillions of Dollars, who are at the Heart of the American Dream, which is to make almost everyone into a Drug Addict, Drunkard, Glutton, Prostitute, Tax Slave, Interest Slave, Insurance Slave, Childcare Slave, and Work Slave, which has Proven to be very Successful in **"The Divided States of United Lies,"** which can Boast about several World Records — such as the Most Rapes, Most Teenage Pregnancies, Most Unwed Mothers, Most Crimes, Most Prisoners, Most Unsolved Murders, Most Drug Addicts, Most Alcoholics, Most Obese People, Most Spoiled Children, Most Indebted People, Most Hospitalized People, Most Medical Doctors, Most Nurses, Most Sold Drugs, Most House Fires, Most Deaths from House Fires, Most Destructions from Tornadoes, Most Expensive Funerals, Most Mass Shootings, Most Unhappy People, Most Suicides, Most Aborted Babies, Most Pot Holes in the Highways, Most Traffic Accidents, Most Gasoline Wasted, Most Foods Wasted, Most Clothing in Closets (most of which is seldom if ever Worn), and the List could go on and on: beCause Americans are Record Breakers. †§‡

06-02 [_] O Elected King, just for the Fun of it, how about a Political Debate between you, Hilarious Clinton, and Donald Trumpeter? For Example, I will be Moderator, who Asks the Important Questions, and each of you give your Responses, no matter how much Time you take to Respond.

06-03 [_] **Moderator:** Please give to the whole World your Best Solution for Unemployment and Underemployment, Worldwide, beginning with Hilarious Clinton.

> A-[_] **Hilarious Clinton:** I Believe that as a Presidential Candidate for the United States of America, it is no Concern of mine how Mexicans, Guatemalans, Hondurans, nor any other Nation of People South of the Border go about making themselves Trillions of Dollars in Debt, like us Americans, who Live in the Greatest Nation on the Earth, which is only 147 Trillion Dollars in Debt to Lying Red Jew Bankers, which is enough Money, if Stacked Up in 100$ Paper Bills, to reach half way to the Moon! Frankly, *their* False Economies Depend on our Great False Economy, which Depends on the Exploitations of the Natural Resources of the Earth, which are somewhat Limited; but, not so Limited that everyone could have a Tarpaper Shanty to Live in, and a 20-feet by 20-feet Garden, which would Cost no less than 200,000$. †§‡

B-[_] **Donald Trumpeter:** To be Perfectly Honest with you, I have never Thought about the Employment of People in Foreign Countries, and especially the Employment of any People in the Middle East, who have almost nothing to Work with, who Live in Worthless Deserts for the most part, who scarcely have enough Water to Wash their Buttockses. Frankly, I have no Idea what do for them; but, I do know how to bring Jobs back to America, by Lowering the Income Taxes for Rich People, who are presently sitting on Trillions of Dollars: because they do not know what to Invest their Money in. After all, it is very Difficult to Compete with those Foreign Workers, who are Contented with only 5$ per Day for their Labors. †§‡

C-[_] **Our Elected King:** I Propose to Establish **"The New RIGHTEOUS One-World Government,"** which will Mint and Print the Necessary New Money — NOT to Give it Away to Ignorant Fools, nor to Pay off National Debts; but, in Order to HIRE whomever is Willing and Able to Learn and Work, in Order to Help Build those **"GLORIOUS Swanky Hotels Castles and Fortresses,"** which will Represent that New Money, which will make it the very Best Money in all of the World. Therefore, we must also Establish **"Seven Great Armies of Working Soldiers,"** in Order to Build those Fortresses most Efficiently, without Wasting any Time, Money, Materials, nor Energy.

06-04 [_] **Moderator:** Does anyone in this Audience have any Objections to the Proposals of our Elected King? If so, please Present those Objections, loud and clear. (No one Objects: beCause of being Afraid that they might be put to Shame for Opening their Mouths.) So, it appears that no one Objects. Therefore, let us go on to the next Question. What is your Best Solution for Gun Violence in our All-American Capitalist Cities?

A-[_] **Hilarious Clinton:** Well, first of all, I would make everyone get a Thorough Background Check before being allowed to Purchase any Deadly Weapons; and secondly, I would Ban all Assault Rifles, which are Designed to Kill other People in Mass Shootings: because they are Military Weapons, which no Civilians need, even if the Federal Government makes War on the Masses of People in America, which it might have to do, just to Maintain Law and Order after I get Elected. After all, many Republicans Vainly Imagine that I am some Kind of a Crook, when I am Actually one of the more Honest Politicians, if you know what I Mean, and certainly more Honest than Billery Clinton, who Lied to the Public about that Lewd-windskee, who seems to have Blown Away, which is rather Sad: because I would have liked to have spent some Time in Bed with her, myself; but, the Opportunity did not Arise. †§‡

B-[_] **Donald Trumpeter:** I would make Sure that our Second Amendment to the Constitution is not Violated by any Means, and thus every American should be Armed with at least 3 Deadly Weapons, just in case there is a Civil War, after I get Elected. After all, I am not very Diplomatic, as Nigger Jim will Gladly Testify in any Courtroom, which is a Shame on me; but, not nearly so Shameful as the Evil Things that I said about Women, in Secret, during my Locker Talk, which did not get Recorded, just Months ago. Indeed, those Dimwitcrats have Justified Reasons for not Wanting to Vote for me, if only they could Hear those Covert Conversations, which Reveal more Truths about me than I care to Confess. Actually, it might be a Good Idea if every Man, Woman, and Child had 5 Weapons, each, just to make Sure that no one is left Alive after that Civil War. †§‡

C-[_] **Our Elected King:** Most of the Gun Violence comes from People who have used Drugs, who probably Learned much of their Violence from Watching Violent Movies, or Playing Violent Video Games. Nevertheless, the Sure Cure for that Problem is to Build those **"GLORIOUS Swanky Hotels Castles and Fortresses,"** whereby no such Weapons are Needed for Self-defense, which could be Locked up in the Castle Armory, if there were any Great Danger of being Attacked by any Foreign Power. After all, it is very Unlikely that Los Angeles is going to make War against Chicago or Houston. Nevertheless, Crazier Things have been done during the Past by Whole Nations of Insane People, as in the Case of the Great American Civil War during the 1860's, which would have also been Prevented by Building those Swanky Fortresses, whereby Slavery would have become Obsolete: beCause Capitalism would have become Obsolete: beCause nearly everyone would have become Moderately Rich, just by Using their Mechanical Slaves to Build those Swanky Fortresses. Therefore, who would have any Need for any Slaves, since there would be X-amount of Voluntary Servants, who would be Happy to do the Gardening, Cooking and House Cleaning, in Exchange for getting to Live within a Swanky Palace, which might Require a Total of an Average of 3 to 4 Hours of Work per Day, in order to Cover all of the Costs for a very High Standard of Living?

06-05 [_] **Moderator:** Does anyone Object to that Plan, which makes it Possible for a Voluntary Working Soldier to Work for 8 Hours per Day, 6 Days per Week, for only 6 Months, and then have the Remainder of the Year Off. Otherwise, a Person could Choose to Work one Day, and have the next Day Off; or, Work one Week, and have the next Week Off; or Work one Month, and then have the next Month Off; or Work for 6 Years, and then have the next 6 Years Off: because it is a very Flexible Plan, According to the Master Plan of our Elected King, who is also Happy to do his Share of the Work that needs doing for making everyone Moderately Rich. Therefore, if there are no Objections, let us go on to the next Question. As the Elected President of **"The New RIGHTEOUS One-World Government,"** what would you do for Solving the Social Security Problem: so that Old People will not have to Worry about their Survival when they get Ready to Retire?

A-[_] **Hilarious Clinton:** Well, I would take Sufficient Tax Money from the Rich Corporations for Supporting all of the Old People, including whatever Money is needed for Health Care for everyone. After all, those Corporations have Trillions of Dollars sitting around in Offshore Banks, right now, which could be used for Raising the Standards of Living for all Old People, who would have more Money to Spend on the Capitalist Trash that is for Sale, which will Help to Fill Up the Trash Dumps: because that is where 99.999,999% of it ends up: because the Great False Economy has no Interest in Producing Good Quality Products that might Endure for 10,000 Years or more. †§‡§§

B-[_] **Donald Trumpeter:** I would Lower the Taxes for all of those Rich Corporations, whereby they might Want to bring their Trillions of Dollars back Home to America, and Spend that Money on Exotic Luxury Cars, Lavish Yachts, and Big Mansions on Hilltops. After all, they Deserve Gold Caskets for their Silver Tombs: because, without them, no one would have any Work of any Kind to do. Therefore, they should be Worshiped as the Saviors of Mankind. Yes, Thank God for Capitalism, which will Prove to be the Financial Salvation of Mankind. Moreover, just to Insure that all Old People have Sufficient Money to Live on when they Retire, they should Buy Stocks and Bonds in the Bubblegum and Balloon Industries, which are likely to POP when **"The New RIGHTEOUS One-World Government"** gets Established: because, who will have any Use for Bubblegum and Balloons, when they could be Riding around in the Clouds of Pride and Vanity in their Golden Chariots with Saints Peter and Paul? †§‡§§

C-[_] **Our Elected King:** I would first of all Invite all of the Young People in the whole World to Join **"The Swanky Associations of Working Soldiers,"** whereby we could Build those **"GLORIOUS Swanky Hotels Castles and Fortresses,"** whereby everyone of them would be Assured of having **"Beautiful Swanky PALACES"** to Live in from the Time that those Palaces get Completed, until they Die, whose Children would Naturally Volunteer to take Good Care of their Parents when they get Old: beCause of being Taught to Honor their Fathers and Mothers, even if they are Cantankerous Snobs, who Despise any Working Soldiers: beCause of Vainly Imagining that they are Superior Beings of the Upper Class, just beCause of Learning a few Sophisticated Words — such as those of Lawyer-craft, Priest-craft, Banker-craft, Medical-craft, Political-craft, or any other Craft, which has given to them that Superiority Complex, which has PUFFED UP their Pride beyond Reason. Indeed, just the Building of those **"Beautiful Swanky PALACES,"** will Greatly Help to Lower their Pride, and make them Respect the Great Creator God, who Provided the Building Materials to Work with, whereby it might be Done. After all, what could be Done without any Water to Work with, for Example? What could be Done without any Metals nor Rocks to Work with? What could be Done without Healthy Working Bodies and Minds? Therefore, seeing that People did not Make nor Create their own Bodies nor Minds, nor anything to Work with, People should Learn to be most Thankful to their Great Creator God for all such Good Things, and thus Learn to be Cooperative with other Voluntary Working Soldiers of Like-mindedness.

06-06 [_] **Moderator:** So, if no one Objects to our Elected King's Master Plan, let us go on to the next Important Question. As an Elected President of the United States of America, what would you do about the National Debt?

A-[_] **Hilarious Clinton:** Well, first of all, I would Try to Cut Government Spending on Wasteful Things — such as the Wars in the Middle East, while letting the Refugees Move into Refugee Camps: because there is no Way that we can Afford to take Good Care of those Refugees, whereby they might be Able to Feed and Clothe themselves. After all, just one Jet Bomber Costs about 260 Million Dollars, which would only Buy 65,000 Concrete Mixing Machines, which would only put 780,000 Young Men to Work with Concrete — that is, IF they had any Sand, Gravel, Water, and Cement to Work with in the Middle East, which might Cost as much as 2 or 3 other Jet Bombers. However, just one of those Bombs Coasts about one million Dollars. Therefore, if they drop 3,000 Bombs per Week, that would amount to no less than 3,000,000,000$, which would be enough Money to Buy all of the Bulldozers, Bucket Loaders, Backhoes, Cranes, Cement, Rocks, Sand, Gravel, Water, Air, Sunrises, Sunsets, Date Palms, Fig Trees, and everything else that might be Needed: beCause they have been Dropping those Bombs for several Years. Therefore, when you Multiply that 3 Billion Dollars, TIMES 300 Weeks, it amounts to no less than 900,000,000,000$, which would be enough Money to Provide those **"Beautiful Swanky PALACES"** for every Person in the Middle East, including

(It is Time for some Sane Person to get Control of this Insane World!)

Osama bin Laden's Widows! After all, there is a Good Chance that 90% or more of those People would just Gladly Volunteer to Build such Palaces, if they were Provided with the Tools to Work with, whereby ISIS (Israeli Secret Instigation Services) could RETIRE, along with Obama has been Osama. In other Words, it is just a Matter of Good Management of the Money. However, for Solving the National Debt Problem, I have no Idea what to do, if all of the Tax Slaves just Stay in Bed, and Refuse to get up and Do anything. Indeed, we are Dependent on them to Pay enough Taxes to Cover all of those Endless Debts, which the Great Grandchildren may not Want to Do! †§‡§§

B-[_] **Donald Trumpeter:** Hilarious Hillary, you are entirely too Crooked to Figure it all Out, which Accounts for your Twisted Tale of Sarcastic Lies. The Best Solution for our National Debt is to Cut Taxes for Rich People: so that they will Invest more Money in America, which can be Earned by the Tax Slaves, Interest Slaves, Insurance Slaves, Drug Slaves, Sex Slaves, Childcare Slaves, and Work Slaves, who will be Happy to be Paid less than Minimum Wages, just to Compete with Cheap Labor in Mexico and China, who are now able to Produce Products at one quarter the Cost, which is making those Governments RICH, which is a BAD Thing: beCause it is not Fair that we should be 147 Trillion Dollars in Debt, while they have Surplus Money to Waste on Air-pollution Controls. Indeed, what we Need to do is get those Coal Mines back into Business, for Producing Clean Coal Energy for Producing more Rusty Steel for making more of those Rusty Cars: so that we can Sell those Cars to those Poor Africans, even if they do not have Interstate Highways to Drive them on: beCause they need to Experience the American Dream, which will become an American Nightmare when all of the Gas and Oil have been Burned Up, which will make our Great Grandchildren Extremely HAPPY! However, those little Bastards do not Deserve to have the Blessings of us Tax Slaves, Interest Slaves, Insurance Slaves, Debt Slaves, Sex Slaves, Drug Slaves, Childcare Slaves, nor Work Slaves, who must now have at least 6 Part-time Jobs, just to Pay the Endless Bills. For Example, Americans Buy their Houses at least 7 Times, while those Ignorant Mexicans Buy their Houses only ONE Time, and do not even have Property Taxes! Indeed, we are the only Free Nation on the whole Earth! Yes, we are Free to Visit the Friendly Banker, in order to Borrow the Necessary Money for Buying a House; and then we are Free to Pay that Friendly Banker enough Interest Money to Pay for that House no less than 2 or 3 Times, and especially if we Mortgage the House for sending the Children to College, whereby they might get a Good Education, which Teaches them that they are the only Free People in the World; and then we are Free to Pay the Property Taxes on the House, whereby we might Buy it once again, or even twice, if we Happen to be in just the Right Location; and then we are Free to Pay for Repairs Bills on the Wooden / Plastic Firetrap Mouse-infested Cockroach Den, which never Cease: beCause, the Way that those Houses are Designed, they Automatically Require Constant Repairs, if only to Rip Up the Stinking Vermin-filled Carpets, and Replace them with New Odious Plastic Carpets, which make the Air almost as Clean as it might be in the New Jerusalem that is coming down from God in the Sky, which Scientists have Spotted in their Telescopes; but, it is Classified as Top Secret, which was Revealed in one of those E-mail Letters to Hilarious Hillary, which was Hacked into by those Ruskies, who Glommed onto the Idea, and took up Bible Studies, and particularly *Revelation 21,* which Inspired them to Want to Build **"The Great World TEMPLE of PEACE,"** in Jerusalem: so that they might Watch for that New Jerusalem, which is supposed to be 1,500 Miles HIGH, if you can Believe it! Well, at any rate, if we had that 20 Trillion Dollars that we presently Owe to those Lying Red Jews, we could Build one Fantastic Temple of Peace, and Cover it with Pure Gold! I Mean that we could make it a Mile Tall, and in 600 Great Terraces, stretching out across the Jordan River, and Covering the Mount of Olives, itself, which is only 3 Miles from Jerusalem, which could have a Special Stone Dome Home Built just for Jesus Christ: so that he will not be Homeless when he Returneth. After all, it would be a Great Shame if he had no Place to Live when he Returneth with tens of thousands of his Holy Angels, who would not likely be Interested in Breathing the Foul Air that comes from those Stinking All-American Capitalist Carpets, which are made with Recycled Used Motor Oil, Plastic Trash Bags, Plastic Bottles, and other Plastic Trash, which has Lead, Arsenic, Mercury, Cadmium, and other Highly Toxic Blessings in it! And, at last, we Americans are Free to Eat and Drink all Kinds of Abominations: because Good Foods and Wholesome Natural Drinks cannot be Found in those Gross Grocery Stores, even if you have lots of Money for Buying it. Indeed, I could probably go on for at least another 10 Pages, telling you all about American Freedoms, which you could Meditate on: so as to come to Understand that we are likely the Lowest most Miserable SLAVES in the World, who Live in a Police State, who are FORCED to OBEY, or else end up in some Federal Prison for Maximum Social Security. †§‡§§

C-[_] **Our Elected King:** Well, the most Simple Solution for our National Debts, is to Learn, Believe, Love, and OBEY the Laws of Moses — one of which is to FORGIVE ALL DEBTS, every 50 Years, and Return the Land to the Masses of People, which is called the Great Year of JUBILEE! (See *Leviticus 25,* which is still a Good Plan.)

06-07 [_] **Moderator:** If there are no Objections to our Elected King's Plan for getting Rid of all Debts, we will go on to the next Important Question.

A-[_] I Agree with our Elected King's Plan for getting Rid of all of the Debts; but, I Object to his Jubilee Plan: because I Fail to Understand just HOW the Land will be Returned to the Masses of People? For Example, the Native American Indians might Want Manhattan Island, in New York City, rather than some Worthless Desert in Arizona or Nevada. Therefore, just HOW would that Land be Divided among those Indians?

B-[_] **Hilarious Hillary:** Well, we could Confiscate the Trump Tower, and Divide the Rooms among the Poorest Indians, who could go Fishing in that big Swimming Pool that was built by Larry Silversteen for a Memorial for the Victims of September 11th, 2001, who Probably Wish to God that they had been Living in those **"GLORIOUS Swanky Hotels Castles and Fortresses,"** which would not have been Greatly Effected by any Airplane Crashes: beCause no Airplane could Penetrate a Solid Granite Stone Wall that is 20 feet THICK, nor even 4 feet thick, if it were Backed Up by Rubble Rocks, Sand, Gravel, and Clay between 2 Solid Stone Walls that are 12 feet apart, for a Total of 20 feet. Indeed, such Airplane Crashes might Ruin a Garden or 2; but, they would have no Great Effect on such STRONG Swanky FORTRESSES, which would be Designed to Withstand Atomic Bombs and whatever, which would make all Bombs Obsolete! †§‡§§

C-[_] **Donald Trumpeter:** Well, Crooked Hillary, Larry Silverstiin might Object to your Wicked Plan to make his Memorial Pool into a Fish Aquarium, when it would be Better to make it into a Cesspool for Capitalist Chemicals, which no one Wants in their Foods nor Drinks, which Amount to more than 37 Billion Gallons per Year, Worldwide, which should be Saved to Spice the Foods and Drinks of Jesus Christ and his Holy Angels, when they Return 2,000 Years too Late, who can be Rightly Blamed for not Explaining to us Ignorant Fools just HOW to Establish and Manage **"The New RIGHTEOUS One-World Government!"** After all, Jesus could have Saved us from all of this Capitalist MADNESS, if he had just Returned 1,900 Years Ago! †§‡§§

D-[_] I Object to the Year of Jubilee on Account of the Fact that it is Impossible to Divide the Land among all of the Poor People in an Equitable Way, whereby each Family might have Fertile Land to Work with, just to Grow their own Foods. Therefore, Moses must have been INSANE, or just a Senile Old Man when he wrote *Leviticus 25*. †§‡§§

E-[_] What does our Elected King have to say about that Subject, since he is the Reincarnation of King Solomon, himself?

F-[_] I Fail to Understand what is WRong with putting everyone to WORK, Building those **"GLORIOUS Swanky Hotels Castles and Fortresses,"** *which will Solve no less than 5,000 Major and Minor Problems, including the Climate Changing Problems, the Unemployment Problems, the Underemployment Problems, the Poverty Problems, the Gun Violence Problems, the Terrorist Problems, the Tax Slavery Problems, the Interest Slavery Problems, the Insurance Slavery Problems, the Drug Trafficking Problems, the Drug Slavery / Addiction Problems, the Prostitution Problems, the Hiring and Firing Problems, and the Human Trafficking Slave Trade Problems, among many other Problems!?* Indeed, our Elected King has already Proven within many Inspired Books that his Master Plan is a Revelation from ALMIGHTY GOD, who alone has the Wisdom to Solve our Massive Problems, which he has Revealed to his Selected KING! {See www.Amazon.com for: **"Are we Americans the Most STUPID People who ever Lived!" (HOW Working People can PROSPER and Live in PEACE Under the Rulership of a RIGHTEOUS KING!) By The Worldwide People's Revolution!®** Book 047.

G-[_] God Knows, and all Well-Educated People also Know, that those **"GLORIOUS Swanky Hotels Castles and Fortresses"** are the Best Solution for ALL of our Massive Problems, and the ONE and ONLY Way to Celebrate the Great Year of JUBILEE! Yes, Moses most likely Visualized it, himself; and therefore, he did not bother to Explain just HOW to Divide the Land among ALL of the People, including the so-called "Rich People," who are also Suffering for a Lack of Fresh Clean Air to Breathe, Pure Living Water to Drink, Natural Clothing to Wear, Wholesome Natural Foods to Eat, and SECURE Cities to Live in. Just Listen to the latest News Reports, and Judge for yourself whether or not we Desperately Need those Swanky Fortresses. For Example, just Yesterday, they gave a Report about Billions of Dollars-worth of Damage from a Hurricane, which would have had ZERO Effect on a Swanky Fortress: beCause the Fruit and Nut Trees, Grape Vines and Berry Bushes would be Protected Behind SOLID STONE WALLS! Yes, those Walls could be 50 to 70 feet Tall in Vulnerable Places like Haiti, Cuba, the Dominican Republic, Florida, and the Carolinas, which are forever getting POUNDED by Violent Winds. Otherwise, those People could Move Inland to

Brokelahoma, or Kansassy, where they could Discover the Values of Tornadoes. Otherwise, they could Move to Colorado, New Mexico, or even to Montana and Canada, where there are VAST Wide-open Spaces of Under-population. †§‡§§

H-[_] HUMBUG! The Cubans are NOT Welcome in **"The Divided States of United Lies!" (The so-called "United States of North America" in Disguise!):** beCause those Cubans are COMMONists, being Worse than the First Church of Christ in *Acts 4—7*, who also had that same False Doctrine, who Vainly Imagined that they could Live on the Accumulated Wealth of whomever Joined their Church, which might have been Okay for a few Years; but, after awhile they Discovered that all such Wealth simply Vanished, and the Apostle Paul had to take up Donations for the Poor Christians in Jerusalem. (See *Second Corinthians 11:8 and Related Scriptures.*)

I-[_] I Object to our Elected King's Master Plan: beCause I am an Innocent Lamb of God, who does not Need nor Desire any **"Beautiful Swanky PALACES"** to Live in: beCause I am Patiently Waiting for the New Jerusalem to come down from Heaven, to the Renewed Earth, which will be AFTER the Thousand Year Reign of Jesus Christ, during which Time we will all Learn our Lessons, one of which is to LOVE our Naaberz as much as we Love ourselves, which is the Anti-thesis of Capitalism, which is to Legally Rob our Naaberz for as much as we can get, which Produces Legal Criminals like Donald Trumpeter and Hilarious Hillary and Bill Adulterous Lying Clinton, who are near Relatives of Bill Computer Software Gates, Incorporated, who Charge 400$ or more for a Computer Disk that Costs only 25 Cents: beCause BILL is a Greedy Selfish Son of SATAN, in my Honest Opinion. †§‡§§

J-[_] Justice Demands that Capitalism must be put on Trial at: **"The Great Worldwide TELEVISED Court HEARING,"** whereby we might Discover just how many High-ranking Criminals it has Produced for the Bernie Madoff and Judas Iscariot Club? Remember that Crimes went Up by 7000% in Moscow, just after those Russians got their DUMBmocracy and Capitalism during the 1990's.

K-[_] King Jesus will take Care of Capitalism, Communism, Socialism and Fascism when he Returns with Power and Great Glory in the Awesome DARK Rolling Clouds of a FEARSOME Sky, along with tens of thousands of his Holy Angels, who will be Zipping all about in their Flying Saucers! Yes, they will be Gathering Up his Elected Servants, and Transporting them into his Great Spaceship, which will be no less than 3 Miles Long, and a half-mile Wide and High, with Various Colors of Flashing Lights, which will be Flying around the World in just one Day, whereby all of the Saints might be Gathered Up; and then the Whole Earth will be Purified by an Unquenchable FIRE, while King Jesus and his Followers will Escape to Mount Zion. Therefore, all of the Evil Works of Unholy Men shall be Destroyed, all around the Earth; and after that the Land will be Divided among all of the Saints, who will Build those **"GLORIOUS Swanky Hotels Castles and Fortresses!"** Yes, they will Inherit the Earth, and make it a Good Place for everyone to Live, after that. †§‡§§

L-[_] Lots of Laughs! Who Dreamed up such Religious Nonsense? It should be Against the Law to Publish LIES! †§‡

(It is Time for some Sane Person to get Control of this Insane World!)

M-[_] How much Money was he Paid for Dreaming up such Religious Nonsense? Indeed, I have Heard Rumors that our Elected King has already Raked in Billions of Dollars from the Sales of all such Nonsense, which is HOW he got enough to Money to Build his own Million-dollar Mansion with the Marble-faced Walls. Indeed, that is WHY he Offers anyone 90% of the Net Profits from the Sales of his Uninspired Books! †§‡§§

N-[_] It is NOT Religious Nonsense! It is the Pure Word of the Living God, which is ONE Word, which is JESUS, who is our Elected KING! Yes, you might find that Difficult to Believe; but, I Ask you, WHO else has Reasonable Solutions for ALL of our Massive Problems? †§‡

O-[_] I Object, your Honor — there is NO Proof that Swanky Fortresses will Solve any of our Massive Problems: because no such Fortresses have ever been Built! No, not even the Neuschwanstein Castle in Southern Bavaria could Withstand an Atomic Bomb; but, the Pantheon in Rome could, and already has Withstood Cannon Balls! †§‡§§

P-[_] Many Ignorant People will Agree with you: beCause they have not Personally Seen **"The Secret City of the Great King,"** which is Hidden in the Recesses of the Uttermost Parts of the Far North, within the Hollow Earth, which is a Paradise, which God has Preserved for Patient Persistent People who become HOLY, even as he is Holy! {See: **"HOW to Become a HOLY Man!" (40 Good Reasons WHY People Should FAST and PRAY!) By The Worldwide People's Revolution!® Book 045.**}

Q-[_] The Great Question is this: **"Can we Ignorant People Possibly Construct anything so Marvelous as Mount Zion, which Shines with the Glory of the Gods?"** I Seriously Doubt it; but, we can at least Learn a few Important Things while Trying.

R-[_] I am Ready to give it a Test.

S-[_] Saint Peter is also Ready, along with all of the other Saints. Indeed, we could call it the New Jerusalem, and Build it in the Great State of Flexible Texas, just for the Fun of it, and Build **"The Great World TEMPLE of PEACE"** in the Middle of it, in the Sixth Court. †§‡

T-[_] That Great Temple can only be Built in the Old Jerusalem: because Jesus will not Return to a Place that he is not Familiar with, which would make him Feel Uncomfortable. †§‡

U-[_] I Understand that Jesus is Flexible, and does not Care which Nation Accepts his Inspired Words of Provable Truths, who would be Greatly Blest for Building such a Great Temple for him, even if it were in Africa or Siberia. Perhaps that Explains why we can find Great Temples in India? †§‡

V-[_] I am a Victim of Capitalism; and therefore, I cannot Visualize **"The END of CONFUSION!" (The Great CELEBRATION of the Wedding of the Humble Honest Nations, and the Grand Year of JUBILEE!) By The Worldwide People's Revolution!®** Book 050. Indeed, it is Incomprehensible to me.

W-[_] It might Require another World War, just to Humble us enough to Agree with our Selected King, whom God has Selected to Govern us: beCause he has found him Worthy.

X-[_] X-amount of People will Accept it, and X-amount will Reject it; but, the Wise People will DEMAND: **"The Great Worldwide TELEVISED Court HEARING,"** whereby the whole Truth might be Discovered about all Important Subjects, including the Flat Earth Theory, which has an Astounding Amount of Physical Proof in Favor of it. †§‡ (See YouTube Videos for the Flat Earth Beliefs, which Refute Modern Science.)

Y-[_] YouTube Videos cannot be Trusted. I would not put any Stock in any of them, and especially those Videos that Debunk the Moon Landings, which are Trying to Confuse us with the FACTS! †§‡§§

Z-[_] The ZEAL of **The Worldwide People's Revolution!®** will make it Possible to Discover the Whole Truth about all Important Subjects. Just be Patient, and keep on Reading.

06-08 [_] **Moderator:** Okay, let us Move On with the next Question, since the Previous Question will have to be Answered at: **"The Great Worldwide TELEVISED Court HEARING,"** which is also True of many other Important Subjects. What is your most Reasonable Solution for Refugees throughout this World of Woes?

A-[_] **Hilarious Hillary:** We have already Concluded that the most Reasonable Solution for all of those Refugees, Migrant Workers, Illegal Immigrants, and other Victims of Capitalism is to Help them to Build those **"GLORIOUS Swanky Hotels Castles and Fortresses,"** which can only be Done if we Tax Slaves Establish: **"The New RIGHTEOUS One-World Government!"** {See: **"AIIRMWVC and Reasonable Solutions!" (Aliens, Illegal Immigrants, Refugees, Migrant Workers and other Victims of Capitalism!) By The Worldwide People's Revolution!® Book 032.**}

B-[_] **Donald Trumpeter:** I am Sorry to say that I have not yet Studied those Inspired Books, whereby I might Know the Truth of it; but, I am beginning to Submit to: **"The Swanky Sword of Divine Truths!"** Yes, it is the Most Powerful Weapon in all of the World, which I did not know Existed, until Today. Sorry about that.

C-[_] **Our Elected King:** Well, now that you have Discovered **"The Swanky Sword of Divine Truths,"** it is Wise of you to Shut your Mouth in all Public Debates, until after you have Studied ALL of my Inspired Books, whereby you might Speak the TRUTH, the Whole Truth, and nothing but the Truth, and Stop Condemning those Poor Mexicans, whom you and other Greedy Selfish People have Branded as "Illegal Aliens," who were too Poor to come to America, Legally, who were the most Poor Ignorant People, who only Wanted to Raise their Standards of Living, who did not Realize that most Americans are nothing but SLAVES — such as Tax Slaves, Interest Slaves, Insurance Slaves, Drug Slaves, Childcare Slaves, and WORK SLAVES, who would give anything to be FREE with a Capital F, even as many Mexicans are Free, who can Set Up Shops along the Streets without even being Taxed for it, unless they have more than 6 Employees, and a certain Income. †‡

(It is Time for some Sane Person to get Control of this Insane World!)

D-[_] **DUMBmocracy:** I must Confess that we Americans have been Greatly Deceived by that Wicked WICKED Anti-Christ FALSE Cover-up Federal Government, which has most of us Worshiping a Bloody RAG, and Pledging our Allegiance to it, when we should be Pledging our Allegiance to our Creator God, ONLY, who Commands us to CELEBRATE the Great Year of JUBILEE, by Forgiving ALL Debts, and Returning the Land to the Masses of People, who can Claim their own Rivers of Water, Lakes, Mountains of Rocks, Minerals, Coal, Oil, Gases, and whatever is Available to Use WISELY, by Establishing **"The New RIGHTEOUS One-World Government,"** which has a **"FREEDUM uv SPEECH Speshoul Maguzeen uv Onust Upinyunz,"** whereby anyone may Express his or her Honest Opinions, Free of Charge, which may be Studied on the Internet by whomever is Interested, whereby DUMBmocracy can at last Freely Speak for itself. †§‡

E-[_] I am Educated enough to Know that no one on this Earth is Able to Read a Billion Ridiculous Opinions in an Endless Magazine of Pure Nonsense! †§‡

F-[_] I Fail to Understand WHY anyone would have a Ridiculous Opinion to Publish, after Studying the Inspired Books of our Faithful Elected King, who has already Answered most of our Questions in his Strange Way, which Causes us to THINK, which Helps us to Remember. Indeed, during the Future, when the Master Index is Finished, everyone will be Able to Discover the Answers to all of their Questions by Means of their Computers. However, if they cannot Find those Answers, they may Address their Important Questions to: **"FREEDUM uv SPEECH!"** (U Speshoul Maguzeen uv Onust Upinions!) By The Worldwide People's Revolution!®, Book 030-0002, which will be Directed to **"The New RIGHTEOUS One-World Government,"** which will have a Staff of Secretaries that will be Able and Willing to Discover the Correct Answers. †§‡

G-[_] God Knows that it is Impossible to Answer all of the Ridiculous Questions that Ignorant People can Ask. For Example, will there be any Swanky Fortresses for Dimwitcrats to Inherit? Or, will they all be Converted into Reprobates or Independent Jackasses? Personally, I am a Gnostic.

H-[_] Honesty and Humility would Cause you to Confess that the Material World is Equally as Important as the Spiritual World, when it comes to Living a Good Life. After all, how can a Person be very Spiritually-minded while he or she is Starving to Death? Moreover, how can a Person be Happy when the Roof just got Blown Off of her House? How can a Person be Healthy, while Eating from Dumpsters? Everyone Knows how Happy he or she is, just to get some Money, and especially a LOT of Money, whereby he or she might Pay the Bills, and have some Extra Money for taking a Vacation! Indeed, when Hopes are Fulfilled, People are made Happy by it, and especially when their Hopes are to make other People Happy by Sacrificing for them, whereby everyone is made Happy by it.

I-[_] Innocent People are just Naturally Healthy and Happy: beCause they Keep their Minds on All that is GOOD, which is GOD. Therefore, STOP Thinking EVIL.

J-[_] We are Justified by our Faith in Jesus Christ, who was not a Rich Person, who most Certainly did NOT Live in any Marble Palaces, even though *Psalm 48* would Lead a Person to Believe otherwise. †§‡

K-[_] King Jesus was Living in a Swanky Palace before he was Born over there in Bethlehem, who was Born to Show to us a Good Example of HOW we should all be Living, if we Want his same Good Reward in the Holy Kingdom of All that is Good, which does Require much Faith, Hope, Trust, Love, Patience, Persistence and Obedience.

L-[_] Lots of Laughs! I can go along with most of it, except the Obedience Part, which would Require that I should Love and Obey his Commandments — one of which Requires me to Lay Down my Life for him, which I am not Willing to do: beCause Life is far too Short to Waste it on Religious Superstitions — such as going to Heaven as a Laughing Hyena. †§‡§§

M-[_] All that I Want is more Money to Buy the Things that make me Happy — such as Booze, Wild Women, Hot Rods, and Big Footballs to Match. Indeed, I am most Happy in a Tent with a Hairy Bear in the Mountains, if you know what I Mean. †§‡

N-[_] Not everyone is Happy with the same Amount of Wealth. Not everyone is Happy with a Boring Job; but, some People are. Therefore, to each his own. Indeed, if you Want to Live like a Beggar, and Sleep in Back Alleys, and Eat from Dumpsters, you are Free to do that; but, I would Prefer to be Moderately RICH, and have an Abundance of every Good Thing, which everyone can have: beCause this World is Blest with hundreds of thousands of Mountains of Rocks, which only need to be Managed Properly, while there is still Plenty of Fuel for Energy to Do that. †§‡

O-[_] I am of the Opinion that our Elected King is the most Sane Person among us, who Understands what MODERATE Means. Therefore, his House is only as Big as it Needs to be for a Family of 6 People, whereby each Person has a Private Bedroom and Bathroom, who Share the Remainder of the House, which has 22 Rooms and a large Porch, which is 70 feet long, and 14 feet wide. In other Words, it is Comfortable, and has Space for Visitors and Storage Rooms. Yes, it is Modest, when Compared with most Mansions. However, when Compared with the little Family Mud Huts in Africa and India, it is Extravagant! Therefore, what are the Options? HOW can we Please everyone?

P-[_] Most People would be Happy to Live in our Elected King's Palace, even though it is NOT a *Swanky* Palace by any Means, which would have to Include all of the Wonderful Things that are Listed in: **"The Environmentalists' Paradise!" (HOW almost Everyone could be Living in a Beautiful Manmade Paradise!) By The Worldwide People's Revolution!® Book 035.**

Q-[_] The Great Question is this: **"Does our Good Earth have all of the Necessary Building Materials for everyone to become Moderately RICH, within those 'Beautiful Swanky PALACES!'?"** And I would say that it does. ‡

(It is Time for some Sane Person to get Control of this Insane World!)

R-[_] Actually, in Reality, the Earth has Plenty of Building Materials and Space for no less than 100 Times as many People, who will have to Learn HOW to Manage their Water: so as to not be Wasting it on the Production of Automobiles, and Raising Cattle for Eating: because, just one Milk Cow can Drink up 50 Gallons of Water per Day, while a Nanny Goat might Drink only 2 Gallons, and Produce a quarter as much Milk! †‡

S-[_] I Propose that we figure out HOW to Transform Ocean Water into Drinking Water, by Feeding that Ocean Water to Coconut Trees, which Thrive along Beaches around the World, which can have Swanky Fortresses built a thousand Feet from the Beaches, even if Hurricanes Blow those Trees over, now and then, which can be Stood Up again with Cranes. Some Trees are more Tolerant of Salty Water than others. It could also be that Salty Water is Neutralized by running it through enough Sand. It needs to be Scientifically Experimented with. Perhaps Seaweeds would Remove enough Salt to make it "Drinkable" by Coconut Trees. ‡

T-[_] People have already Tested everything that they can Think of, and no Rational Conclusions have been drawn up for HOW to make Fresh Water from Sea Water — except that Solar-powered Water Distillers are somewhat Practical for Oil-rich Nations, like Saudi Arabia. Chances are that there is a Simple Solution. ‡

U-[_] I Understand that our Elected King has the Best Solution, which is to Save the Fresh Water that is now Running Away into the Oceans. For Example, the Mighty Amazon River runs out more than a Trillion Gallons per Day, which is going to Waste: because it could be Saved and Used Wisely. ‡

V-[_] Being Victims of Capitalism, we Human Beings are Unlikely to ever Work Together with United Effort, whereby we might all Prosper Properly. †§‡

W-[_] I would rather go to War, than to Cooperate with those Russians, Chinese, Indians, and Africans, who can Fix their own Problems. †§‡

X-[_] X-amount of Ignorant People will Agree with you, without Understanding that except for the Grace of God, we could all be in Worse Conditions by a hundred Times.

Y-[_] I am Yearning for the Happy Day when all People Learn to Work Together with United Effort, like the Amish People who Build Barns and Houses.

Z-[_] The Zeal of **The Worldwide People's Revolution!®** will make that Possible.

06-09 [_] **Moderator:** What are your Thoughts about Reparations for the Poor Mistreated African-Americans, who were made into Slaves during the 1700—1800's? Should Reparations be made; and, if so, HOW?

A-[_] **Hilarious Hillary:** Well, it seems to be about 150 Years too Late to be making any Reparations for American Slaves; but, I would not Object to Providing Free College Educations for any Black People who might Apply, even in Africa, where Schooling is most Desperately Needed. However, just Exactly WHO would Pay for all of those

Computers that might Provide such Learning, is a Good Question? Perhaps we could Ask for Voluntary Contributions from Americans who might be Compassionate enough to Donate such Computers. After all, probably not one African in 100 would be Interested in such an Education, including African-Americans; or else the present Computers in Public LIE-braries might be Occupied with such Students. However, they are rather Low-grade Computers, and very Uncomfortable Chairs, which probably Discourage most Students. Therefore, those Students need Swanky Easy Chairs to sit in, and large Wide Flat-Screen Apple Computers with High-speed Internet Connections, plus Ear Phones for Quiet Truth-braries.

B-[_] **Donald Trumpeter:** I Suggest that we gather up all African-Americans and send them back to Africa with a thousand Shiploads of Modern Tools to Work with, whereby they can Build their own **"GLORIOUS Swanky Hotels Castles and Fortresses,"** *if they are Interested in Working for those Good Swanky Wages* — such as 60$ per Hour for Installing the Marble Tiles on the Solid Stone Walls of their own Stone Dome Complexes with million-gallon Cisterns for Water Storage, who can Choose the Best Places in Africa to do their Building, just as long as they Agree to Help those Native Africans to Build their own Swanky Fortresses, whereby they might all Live in Peace with True Prosperity.

C-[_] **Jil Stiin:** You might not have Heard of me, until now; but, I am the Presidential Candidate for the *Green Party,* which could Draw enough Votes away from Hillary: so that Donald might Win the 2016 Election Deception: beCause I Offer FREE College Educations to all Americans, Worldwide, who could get most of their Educations from the Internet, from Video Recordings, which can be Contributed by Professors and School Teachers who have Love and Compassion, who can Live in those **"Beautiful Swanky PALACES,"** just for making their Contributions.

D-[_] **Gary Jonsun:** Hello, I am the Presidential Candidate for the *Libertarian Party,* which is just a little more Popular in America than the *Green Party;* but, neither Party has even the Slightest Chance of Winning the 2016 Election Deceptions: because we were not Allowed to Debate Hilarious Hillary, nor Donald Trumpeter, much less our Elected King, who is Miles and MILES Ahead of all of the Political Parties in this Race to **"The BIG White OUTHOUSE on the Not-so-Biblical Capitol DUNGHILL!"** After all, he has the Great Advantage of having **"The Swanky Sword of Divine Truths"** on his Side, which makes me look Incredibly Silly and very Selfish. For Example, I was about to Suggest that all African-Americans Band Together in some Sweaty Swamp like Southern Mississippi, and Build a very large Swanky Fortress for ALL African-Americans, whereby they might Prove once and for all Time that they are not Able to Govern themselves without the Help of White People, which has already been Proven in Africa, and hundreds of Years Ago, when Africans were Gathering Up other Africans to Sell as Slaves to those Lying Red Jews, who Controlled the Slave Market, who Owned most of the Ships, and who Gained most of the Money at the Auction Blocks in America. However, now that I have Thought about it, I have Retracted that Proposal: because the Hot Humid State of Mississippi is NOT an Ideal Place to Build a Swanky Fortress, and neither is any Swamp in Africa. However, there are certain Places over there that would be Idea for Building Fortresses, which should be Investigated: beCause it is Possible to Help those Poor People to Prosper in a Good Way, even if they Need the Assistance of a

(It is Time for some Sane Person to get Control of this Insane World!)

few White Men, who would likely be Happy to Help them; but, if not, there are likely many Black Americans, who would be Willing to Sacrifice their Time and Energy to Help them to Prove that Black People are Equally as Talented as White People, which would Settle that Racial Issue, once and for all Time. After all, if they are Equal with White People, they should be Able to Build an Equally GLORIOUS Swanky Fortress, just to Prove it. For Example, they could use the Sand in the Sahara Desert to make Glass Dome Home Complexes: beCause Glass is mostly SAND. Moreover, that Sand can be Heated Up by Solar Power, using Mirrors, which could Prove to be a bit Tricky; but, some Black People are very Inventive and Innovative. Therefore, it will be a Test of their Abilities, which will Prove to be most Interesting for those Black Roosters, who get up and Crow about their Equal Rights. In Fact, I dare say that without some Good Preachers among them, they will end up Killing each other, just like they are Presently doing in Chicago. †§‡

E-[_] **Our Elected King:** I say that the Best Form of Reparations is to Offer all Colored Peoples in the whole World an Opportunity to Build their own **"Beautiful Swanky PALACES,"** with the Assistance of **"The New RIGHTEOUS One-World Government,"** which will Snoopervise all Construction Projects, just to make Sure that the Great Great Grandchildren have Good Places to Live. Therefore, each Group of Like-minded People should make their Drawings and Plans for all such **"GLORIOUS Swanky Hotels Castles and Fortresses,"** and Present those Plans to **"The New RIGHTEOUS One-World Government"** for their Approval and Good Advice: because there are certain Building Codes that must be Followed, just to Prevent any Future Disasters. For Example, all Gardens should be Drained into large Cisterns, whereby that Water can be used again and again, rather than Run Off into the Ocean, even though the Oceans do Need some Fresh Water for the Fishes. However, that Water can come from the Lands Outside of Swanky Fortresses, such as the Great Plains, which should be Returned to the American Bisons, Deers, Antelopes, Beavers, and whatever Creatures used to Live there, which will be True Reparations. Meanwhile, all of the Farmers and Ranchers who Give Up their Lands will be Invited to Live in the Swanky Palaces of their Choices with other People of Like-mindedness. ‡

F-[_] I Object, O King, on Account of the Fact that there are no Like-minded People in the whole World, who can all Agree about any given Subjects. For Example, just Listen to the *Washington Journal,* on the C-SPAN Network, and you will Discover what a Great Diversity of Thoughts and Ideas that there are in this World of Wonders. {See: **"The Washington Journal is a FARCE!" (C-SPAN Managers are not very WISE!) By The Worldwide People's Revolution!® Book 006.**}

G-[_] God Knows that **"The Swanky Sword of Divine Truths"** will Unite the Righteous People, who can all Agree to Learn, Believe, Love, and Obey **"The New MAGNIFIED Version of the Ten Commandments,"** which can be Found in: **"LIGHTNING Versus the Lightning Bug!" (HOW almost Everyone can become Moderately RICH, without Telling Any Lies nor Selling Any Trash!) By The Worldwide People's Revolution!® Book 001.**

H-[_] Heaven have Mercy on us — God Knows that not 2 People on this Earth can Agree 100% about any Subject, except that Sunrises and Sunsets can be very Beautiful, Fragrant Flowers are Pleasant to Smell, Fruit Trees are Beautiful, and everyone Loves Innocence. Indeed, most People like Horses; but, not everyone Wants a Horse to Care for it. Most People like Wooden Painted Plastic Houses; but, few of them like the Repair Bills, much less the Work that is Involved in making those Repairs. Most People like Cars; but, few People like Car Accidents, Car Payments, Car Repairs, Car Maintenance, Car Insurance, Pollution, nor any of the Negative Things about Cars; but, how many of them would Agree to Live without any Cars within **"Beautiful Swanky PALACES,"** which have no Need for any Cars? Suppose they Want to take a Family Vacation to some National Park, how are they supposed to get there — in some Underground Subway Bullet Train? How Pleasant would that Trip be? †§‡

I-[_] Once those **"GLORIOUS Swanky Hotels Castles and Fortresses"** are Finished, very few People will have any Great Interest in Leaving them, except to go to some other Glorious Planned City States, which could also be Located within Hiking or Biking Distances of National Parks, which could have Horses, Camels, Donkeys and Mules for Tourists to Ride. Otherwise, there could be Electric Subway Trains that run to them, as well as Highways for Quadrupeds, which are Quiet and Peaceful and Energy Efficient. Indeed, Voluntary Young Men could Pedal them for Old People, which would be Slow Travelling up Hills and around Mountains; but, at least they would not be Greatly Polluting the Earth. After all, there would not be a Great Rush to get anywhere during those Days: because no one would be put into a Capitalist Pressure Cooker, whereby their Heads might EXPLODE with Anxieties. Besides that, their would be Innocent Deers, Antelopes, Elks, Mooses, and many other Beautiful Animals to View on all such Trips. Moreover, there would likely be Rock Shops and Souvenir Stores along the Way, as well as Rest Rooms and Restaurants for Tourists, at least every 5 to 10 Miles. Such Quadruped Highways and Bike Paths would be in 3 Lanes, having the Middle Lane for Passing, which Highways would likely never Wear Out: beCause of not Running Heavy Trucks and Cars on them. Subway Trains could Transport any Heavy Loads, and even extra Heavy People, if there are any. ‡

J-[_] Justice Demands that Reparations should be made in Cash Payments of a Million Dollars to each Black Person in America. †§‡

K-[_] Kindergarten Children will be able to Understand how Corrupting that Plan might be, seeing that all such Black Children would be Spoiled by such an Act of Generosity, and would likely Waste their Money on Drugs, and at last make Fools of themselves like the Prodigal Son of *Luke 15*.

L-[_] I am Longing for the Day when I can Earn FAIR Swanky Wages for doing Necessary Labor, which will be enough Reparations for me. {See: **"A List of FAIR Swanky Wages!" (The Equitable Wage System!) By The Worldwide People's Revolution!**® Book 065.}

M-[_] My Mother Lived and Died in a State of Extreme Poverty for the Lack of **"The New RIGHTEOUS One-World Government!"** Moreover, she was not Black, Brown,

(It is Time for some Sane Person to get Control of this Insane World!)

Gray, Yellow, Red, Blue, Green, nor Purple; but, she was WHITE. Moreover, she Worked 12 to 16 Hours every Day, and without any Pay: beCause she was a General Slave — Thanks to Capitalism and Vain Traditions, which we must Change, just to have some True Justice for the Masses of People in this World of Woes, which Begins with a Righteous Monetary System, whereby all Money must be Earned by Honest Labor, without any Bankers, without any Loans, without any Interest, and without any Taxes: beCause that is HOW Jesus Christ would Operate his Good Government. †‡

N-[_] Almost no one on this Earth has been Treated Fairly since the Beginning of Time; but, now it is Possible and most Practical for almost everyone to be made Moderately RICH!

O-[_] Are there no Options? Can we not Choose to be Poor and Miserable? Whatever Happened to DUMBmocracy?

P-[_] Most People would Gladly Choose to become Moderately Rich, which was not Practical, until NOW, when we have Mechanical Slaves that can do most of the Work for us, whereby it is now Possible for almost everyone to become Moderately RICH, if they are Willing to Learn and Work, which most People are. Yes, just Ask them, if you Doubt it. Moreover, they will not Need a College Degree of any Kind to Build those Beautiful Planned City States: beCause there are already enough Educated People for doing it. †§‡

Q-[_] The Great Question is: **"Will Black People have anything to Complain about, if we Establish 'The New RIGHTEOUS One-World Government!'?"** Indeed, their Reparations will Automatically be taken Care of by that Act of Congress: beCause they will get to Build their own **"Beautiful Swanky PALACES!" (A New Concept in Living Habits — Swanky Palaces for Poor People!) By The Worldwide People's Revolution!® Book 066.**

R-[_] That will be Sufficient Reparations for me, which is WHY that I have Checked this Box [_] and the above Box, and have Printed and Signed my Name below with the Date:

S-[_] I Refuse to make a SLAVE of myself, just to Help Build any Swanky Palace for myself, which might Require 20 Years of Hard Labor, along with the Assistance of: **"Seven Great Armies of Working Soldiers!" (HOW to Provide a Way for Everyone to WORK: so as to Eliminate Poverty, Crimes, Drug Abuses, Prisons and Unnecessary Taxes!) By The Worldwide People's Revolution!® Book 015.**

T-[_] I will be Happy to Testify in a Courtroom that Reparations are Necessary for the American Indians, the Peoples of the Philippines, Japan, Germany, France, Cambodia, Laos, Vietnam, Korea, Afghanistan, Iraq, Libya, Egypt, Syria, Jordan, Palestine, Lebanon, Grenada, Panama, Colombia, Venezuela, Mexico, Guatemala, Honduras, El Salvador, Costa Rica, Bolivia, Peru, Ecuador, Brazil, Paraguay, Uruguay, Argentina, Cuba, and wherever we Americans have Mistreated Poor Ignorant People, and have taken

Advantage of them for our own Gain, by Capitalist Exploitations, which were Inspired by the Satanic Version of the Holy Bible, which did not make it Clear what it Means to Love our Naaberz as much as we Love ourselves, which would most Certainly not Include EXPLOITING them for our own Gain, whereby we might make Enemies of them, and thus Promote those Hateful WARS! †§‡

U-[_] I Understand that many People around the World have been Mistreated by many Aggressive Nations and Evil Empires; but, all of those Evil Things were done during the PAST, which must be Forgiven and Forgotten, in Order for People to be Mentally Healed by any Means. However, in Order to have True Justice for all Peoples, it is now Time to Offer the Services of **"The New RIGHTEOUS One-World Government!" (HOW to Establish a Righteous One-World Government without Going to WAR!) By The Worldwide People's Revolution!®** Book 056.

V-[_] I am a Victim of Capitalism and the Propaganda Lies thereof; and therefore, I have no Idea what to Do about Reparations for all of the Mistreated People in this World of Woes; but, I do Know that there will be no Peace, just as long as People Believe that they have not been Treated Justly, which is the Case for most Minority Groups of People. ‡

W-[_] World Wars have broken out beCause of those Injustices. Therefore, it is Extremely Important for us Earthlings to get our Act Together, and make Reparations by Providing a Way for almost everyone to become Moderately RICH, if they are Willing and Able to Learn and Work. Otherwise, if Young Men and Women are DRAFTED as Working Soldiers, in Order to Build **"Beautiful Swanky PALACES"** for the Elite Class, who do nothing to Assist those Working Soldiers, they will Think of themselves as Common SLAVES for Unjust Masters, whereby they will also become Unhappy, and thus Unhealthy, Depressed, Mean, and Miserable — all for the Lack of **"The New RIGHTEOUS One-World Government!"** ‡

X-[_] X-amount of People will Agree with you — that it would be WRong to Draft Working Soldiers, and Pay them Minimum Wages for doing Maximum Amounts of Hard Labor, as if going to War, whereby those Young People would only be Abused, once again. However, if all of those Young People are HIRED with Fair Swanky Wages to Help Build their own **"Beautiful Swanky PALACES,"** they will Naturally LOVE it: beCause of getting to Move into their own Palaces, which they will be Happy to take Good Care of, and not allow them to become Trash Dumps like Niggerville, Haiti. †§‡

Y-[_] Yes, I Agree with you — that those Voluntary Working Soldiers would take Personal Interests in Building their own **"Beautiful Swanky PALACES,"** if such a Thing is Possible, which would Naturally Depend on whether or not we Tax Slaves are Able to Establish **"The New RIGHTEOUS One-World Government!"**

Z-[_] The Great ZEAL of **The Worldwide People's Revolution!®** will make that Possible and most Practical.

06-10 [_] **Moderator:** Our next Question concerns Police Brutalities in America, which is mostly an American Problem, which is seldom Experienced in Nations that are either Totally

(It is Time for some Sane Person to get Control of this Insane World!)

Mongrelized or all of one Basic Color. For Example, Police Brutalities are not Major Issues in most European Nations, which are more Civilized. However, all Major Cities in the World have a certain Amount of Corruption in their Governments, including their Police DEPARTments, which would not be Necessary within those **"GLORIOUS Swanky Hotels Castles and Fortresses,"** which are Designed for RIGHTEOUS People, who have Filled Out and Filed **"The Complete SURVEYS of our VALUES!" (SURVEYS of Religious Spiritual Political Governmental Sexual Social Moral Economic Business Labor Habitual and Miscellaneous VALUES!) By The Worldwide People's Revolution!®** Book 059. Indeed, what Need would there be for Peaceable Christians to have Police DEPARTments, seeing that they could easily Discover any Rebel Children, and get them Corrected or Banished from their Cities?

A-[_] **Hilarious Hillary:** I cannot Imagine HOW we could Separate the Good People from the Bad People: beCause there are normally Good and Bad People within the same Family. For Example, I know of a certain Family that has 2 Bad Boys and 3 Good Boys, who were all Raised and Taught the same Sunday School Lessons, who were Forced to Attend Church Services with their Parents, which seemed to make 2 of those Boys into Rebels: beCause they were Born Rebels, you might say, who had no Interest in Sunday School Classes, much less in Boring Religious Services about Sacrifices, Sanctifications, Justifications, and all such Adult Spiritual Subjects, who should have been Excused from Attending any such Services: beCause the Sermons were far Beyond their Abilities to Comprehend them. However, as for Police Brutalities in America, it is like Training Dogs to get along Well with Cats that they were not Born nor Raised with, who are at Odds with one another, who can never get Along Well. Nevertheless, if the Potential Police are Raised within the Community that they will Police during the Future, there is a much Greater Possibility that they will get Along Well with their Friends and Naaberz, than if they are Total Strangers: because they have some Things in Common. Therefore, if those Police have Good Personalities, and do their Best to make Friends with the People that they Police, they will all get Along much Better. However, if only the Mean Boys and Girls become Police, there are bound to be Future Troubles among them. Therefore, there needs to be some Screening Process, whereby any Potentially Bad Policemen can be Discovered and Directed toward the Fire DEPARTment, or the Sewage System Janitors. Otherwise, I have no Idea what to Do about Police Brutalities. †§‡

B-[_] **Donald Trumpeter:** What those Niggers need is Matt Dillon of Dodge City to Correct them, who is Big and Tough enough to Bully them Properly, whereby they might have Respect for him, even if they do not Love him. Personally, I would Beat the Hell Out of them when they first Crossed the Line, and Joined some Gang of Outlaws — such as Hell's Angels on Motorcycles, who Think of Women as Toys to be Used and Abused. Otherwise, I have no Idea what do about those Niggers. †§‡§§ {See: **"For the Love of Money!" (The Strange Things that People Say and Do to Get more Money!) By The Worldwide People's Revolution!®**, Book 003, which contains a Special Chapter called: **"Nigger Jim Explains what a True Nigger IS!"** Hint: Donald Trumpeter is a White Nigger in the Eyes of most Black People and Honest White People and Intelligent Brown People. Indeed, he and O. J. Simpleton are 2 of the same Kind of Psychopathic Liars.}

C-[_] **Our Elected King:** The Moderator is Correct — that **"GLORIOUS Swanky Hotels Castles and Fortresses"** will have no Need for any Policemen: beCause they will only be Inhabited by Righteous People, who alone will Qualify for our Help, who only have to Agree to Learn, Believe, Love, and OBEY **"The New MAGNIFIED Version of the Ten Commandments,"** which you can find in: **"LIGHTNING Versus the Lightning Bug!" (HOW almost Everyone can become Moderately RICH, without Telling Any Lies nor Selling Any Trash!) By The Worldwide People's Revolution!®** Book 001. Therefore, for all such Wise People, those Police Brutalities will CEASE. Indeed, all of the Stupid Ignorant People, who Love Capitalist Greed and Corruption are Welcome to Remain in their Cities of Confusion, where the Policemen are likely to become more and more Brutal, and Especially when all of the Righteous People DEPART from their Cities of Confusion, and go to Work with **"The Swanky Associations of Working Soldiers!" (A Fascinating Collection of Various Kinds of Voluntary Working Soldiers!) By The Worldwide People's Revolution!®** Book 018. Indeed, if those Police get Mean Enough, those Brutalized People will finally Wake Up and Join **"The New RIGHTEOUS One-World Government!"** Yes, it will no doubt Cross their Minds that it is Better for them to be Good Law-abiding Citizens, who Live Simple Lives within those **"GLORIOUS Swanky Hotels Castles and Fortresses!" (Beautiful Planned City States for WISE Intelligent Well-Educated People with Common Sense and Good Understanding!) By The Worldwide People's Revolution!®** Book 019.

D-[ ] **Jil Stiin:** I have no Idea what to say about that Subject: because it is Over my Head. Indeed, I cannot Comprehend just HOW a City of Confusion could Function at all without a certain Number of Righteous People to Manage it. Therefore, if all of the Righteous People have DEPARTED from all Cities of Confusion, there will be nothing but Criminals left in them, who will likely Destroy each other, which is Okay with me. †‡

E-[ ] **Gary Jonsun:** I Wish to God that I had Thought of the Good Ideas that have been Presented by our Elected King. After all, it is Obvious that it is much Easier to Control a Small City of Wise People, than a Monstrous City of Confusion, where no one is in Control, where People are Free to come and go as they Please, who have no Walls nor Gates to Keep Out any Unwanted Creatures, Criminal Characters, Tax Masters, nor Usury Masters. However, most Modern Businesses, Banks, Factories and Corporations do have Fences, Surveillance Cameras, Security Guards, Spies, and other Snoops, who Cost Americans no less than 450 Billion Dollars per Year, which would soon Pay for those Tall Stone Walls around Swanky Fortresses, if that Money were Used WISELY, along with the Energy that is now Wasted in Needless Vehicles. Therefore, I must Confess that our Elected King is in Fact the KING of the Mountain, whom no one is going to Defeat by any Means with his Rubber sword. Moreover, I have no Idea what Libertarians might Think about all such Swanky Fortresses; but, I would Suspect that most of them would draw up Irrational Conclusions before Studying them and their many Great Advantages. {See: **"The Right Design for Living!" (A List of Great Advantages for Building Beautiful Planned City States!),** Book 012, plus: **"The Low Court of Supreme Injustices is Brought to Trial!" (The Worldwide People's Revolution!® Butts Heads with the United States Supreme Court, with or without their Black Robes of Hypocrisies and Lies!),** Book 011, plus: **"Poverty Hunger Riots Strikes Brutalities Election Deceptions and Civil Wars!" (The High Price that we Earthlings** have Paid for Leaving the Good Land!) By The Worldwide People's Revolution!® Book 014.}

06-11 [_] **Moderator:** Our next Question concerns Privacy versus Security. In other Words, is our Privacy of more Importance than our Security; or, is our Security of more Importance than our Privacy??

A-[_] **Hilarious Hillary:** It is our God-given Right to have a certain Amount of Privacy, which is WHY that I had my own Private Server for the Internet in my Basement, when I was Secretary of State, which was without any Doubt the most Foolish Thing that I did during that Time, whereby some Top Secret Classified Information might have gotten into the Hands of our Enemies. For Example, there was an E-mail from the State DEPARTment, stating that ISIS was Actually the Israeli Secret Instigation Services, which, if it had gotten into the Hands of German, French, Chinese, or Russian Intelligence Agencies, might have Proven to be a bit Em-bare-assing for **"The Divided States of United Lies,"** who Work Together with those Israelis to keep the Wars going in the Middle East: beCause it has Proven to be very Profitable for those Lying Red Jew Weapons Manufacturers, Chemical Corporations, Drug Businesses, and especially the Bankers, who Kindly Loan to us Americans Money for making Wars, whereby they Collect Trillions of Dollars for the Interest / Usury on the Loans. Indeed, Jil Stiin has already Informed us that the Wars in the Middle East will Cost us no less than 16 Trillion Dollars, counting the Future Veteran's Expenses and the Long-term Interest on the Loans, which will Require no less than 10,000 Years to Pay Off the Principal on those Loans. Most of the Money is Borrowed by the Federal Government for Buying Military Equipment, Weapons, Bombs, Uniforms, Vehicles, Foods, Transportation in Airplanes, and whatever the Military Needs, which Averages about a Trillion Dollars per Year: because we Maintain more than 800 Military Bases around the World. However, instead of Maintaining some Bases in Iraq, we Withdrew, and left a Vacuum for ISIS / ISIL to Fill, which brought about the Crisis in Syria, Libya, Sudan, Somalia, and Fort Hood, who are Friends with Iran and Russia, who Bomb their own People: beCause they LOVE them, somewhat like Judas Iscariot Loved Jesus, who Symbolizes all Betrayers of Trust, including Donald. Whatever the Case, you might find it most Interesting that the DEPARTment of Defense (DoD), Federal Burden of Investigation (FBI), and the Central Unintelligent Agencies (CIA) have more than 10 Trillion Pages of Top Secret Documents in their Files, much of which is Information about Good Honest Hardworking Americans — such as our Elected King, who does not have a Police Record for anything, which seems to Irritate them: beCause they like to have Control over other People, which they have over most People: beCause of having Inside Information about them and their so-called "Secret Sins," whereby they can Threaten to Expose them, if they do not Cooperate with the Snoops and the Shadow Government, which is run by Lying Red Jews. For Example, they Know that the Pope of Rome had Romantic Affairs during his Younger Days, which would make him Look Bad, if such Information were Leaked, which gives to them Power over him, which is also WHY the Holy Roman Catholic Church has always Chosen someone with "Baggage," as they say, who must Cooperate with the Masters in Charge, who are those Lying Red Jew Bankers, who Control the Money Game, even as they have been for thousands of Years: beCause they are the Money Masters. †§‡§§

B-[ ] **Donald Trumpeter:** I just LOVE that Hilarious Hillary! — that is, Crooked Hillary, who should be Thoroughly Investigated, and Sentenced to 120 Lifetimes of Slave Labor in a Rock Quarry, right next to Bill Adulterous Lying Clinton, who should have a 10-feet-long Pole Locked between their Handcuffs: so that they can never Touch each other; but, so that they have to Pack that Pole around with them at the Rock Quarry, along with their Shackles and Chains: beCause they have been Chief Criminals, and not nearly so Innocent as myself, who had 4,000+ Lawsuits against me, until I Legally went Bankrupt, and Slipped Out from under all of that: because I am Smart. In Fact, I am so Smart that I let my Tongue Hang myself by the Private Parts, you might say, while Talking about those Lewd Women, Beauty Stars, and Slippery Comets, which used to be Dancing around in my Sexual Fantasy World, which Inspired some Locker Room Talk, if ye knoweth what I Meaneth, as Nigger Jim might say it, after Attending some of those Sunday School Classes with Huck Finn and Tom Sawyer and dat thar' Indian, whose Name I cannot Recall — that is, the one who Killed Huck's Pappy. Well, at any rate, now that my Pink Underwear has been Exposed with that of **"The UGLY Scarred Dishonest Face of Poor Old Miserable UNCLE SAM,"** I am left alone to Meditate on our National Security — not that it is in a Grave Danger for any of my Foul Conversations; but, that it is Worrisome to 47% of Americans, who are Worried that they or their Loved ones might be Involved in some Future Terrorist Attacks, in spite of the Fact that ISIS does not Want to take any Chances on Visiting **"The Divided States of United Lies,"** because of the Possibility of getting Water Boarded 183 Times in the Guantanamo Bay Rest Home for Retired Terrorists, in Cuba, which we have Occupied ever since 1830, or thereabouts, having Permission from the Pope of Moscow, if'n ye knoweth what I Meaneth. Well, at any rate, I have always Wondered WHY those Russians did not get a Foothold in Key West, Florida, whereby they might have also Maintained a Military Base in our own Backyard? Moreover, why did the Chinese not Establish a Base in Baja, California, just for their National Security's Sake. Likewise, the North Koreans should have Established a Military Base on Nantucket, in Massivechewshits, when Edward Kennedy was in Charge of Drowning Women in Chapelwicked, or Chappaquiddick, or whatever the Hell it was, after getting Drunk at Gay Bars with John Fitzgerald, who was the Saintly President, who only had 40 Sexual Relations with near Relatives of Marilyn Monroe, who was a Real Looker and Hooker, who let those Nasty Drugs get the Upper Hand on her, which was such a Shame on America: because she could have been our Queen Victoria. Even as it was, she gave to me *the Seven Year Itch* to jump into Bed with her, which I could not get Off of my Mind after Lusting after her, which was not my Fault: beCause it is the Way that God Created me, and with no Warning Signs Attached to my own Buttocks, whereby I might have been more Careful to Avoid the Movies, and Especially those *James Bond 007 Movies,* which Heroized Fornicators like him, and made Smoking and Drinking the Habits of "Good Actors," which was Satan's Way of Perverting America — Thanks to those Red Jew Hollywood Movie Makers, who seem to be Determined to Ruin us; and for what Good Reason, I have no Idea. However, if I am Elected to be the Powerless President, I will Introduce a Bill to Congress to put all of them Out of Business, if they do not Confess their Motives, and come Clean about their Red Jew Scandals, whereby they have Raked in tens of Trillions of Dollars from Lust-filled Young People and even from Old People, who should know by now HOW Satan Manages his Unholy Kingdom! †§‡§§

(It is Time for some Sane Person to get Control of this Insane World!)

C-[_] **Our Elected King:** It has already been made Clear that it is Possible for everyone to have their Privacy and Security within those **"GLORIOUS Swanky Hotels Castles and Fortresses,"** which allow for the Fact that there are X-amount of Horny Trumpeters and Maneuvering Monroes, who are Welcome to Live with Like-minded People; but, not with the Righteous People, who will Check the Appropriate Boxes below:

01-[_] I Believe in Fidelity, which is Sexual Faithfulness to just one other Person, which God Loves and Respects; and so should we.

02-[_] I Believe in Fornicating with James Bond, whenever the Opportunity Arises without any Chances of getting Caught Red-handed by the Federal Burden of Investigation, who are Notorious Fornicators. ‡

03-[_] I Believe that it is none of your Business, nor anyone else's Business, what my Private Sexual Life is about. Indeed, if I want to Whore around Town, that is my Business, alone.

04-[_] I Believe that Jesus Christ would have Checked the First Box, while King David would have Checked the Second Box: because he was a Man after God's own Heart. (See *Acts 13:22*.)

05-[_] I Believe that Jesus Christ would have Checked the First Box, while King David would have Checked the Third Box.

06-[_] I Believe that almost every Man who ever Lived needed to "Sow his Wild Oats," as the Saying goes, which Means that a Man should do enough Fornicating to Discover that it is not nearly as Rewarding as True Love, which Requires Fidelity and someone who Truly Loves you from the Heart for who you are; and not for the Sake of getting your Money nor Property. †§‡

07-[_] I Believe that Young People are Healthier and Happier if they Abstain from having Sex, until they are Mature and Married, which might be 16 Years Old for Boys, and 25 Years Old for Wombmen. †§‡§§

08-[_] I Believe that having Sex is a Sacred Act between a Man and Woman, only, who have been Married to God, who Promise to Love and Obey the Commandments of God, one of which is to Practice Fidelity.

09-[_] I Believe that Gay Young Men should be Married to other Gay Young Men, so as to Avoid Whoredoms — such as Priests having Sex with Altar Boys: beCause it is written, *"Marriage is Honorable in all Cases, even between Men who Love other Men, even as Jesus Loved John, and Jonathan Loved David; and therefore, the Bed of Sensual Pleasures is Undefiled by People who Practice Fidelity: because God Loves Fidelity; but, Whoremongers, Sodomites, and Adulterers will be Judged by the Supreme Judge, who Rewards every Person according to his or her Words and Works." — NMV of Hebrews 13:4.* †§‡

10-[_] I Believe that the Author of this Uninspired Book is CRAZY! †§‡

11-[_] I Believe that Greek Frot Sex is the Supreme Sexual and Sensual Act, which no one has Improved on during more than 2,500 Years, which is only Enhanced by True Love between 2 very Gay Men, who Practice Fidelity, who Understand the Love of God, who is also GAY! †§‡§§ {See: **"How GAY is GOD?" (Oh the Wonders of it all when it all Hangs Out!) By The Worldwide People's Revolution!®**, Book 071, which Cover Photo shows 2 very Gay Dogs.}

12-[_] I Believe that the Creator God is a Different God than the Biblical Hebrew God, who was a bit Confused about Sex and many other Important Issues. †§‡ {See: **"Those Ridiculous Contradictions within the Holy Bible!" (HOW to Read the Mutilated Bible with an Open Mind!) By The Worldwide People's Revolution!®** Book 057.}

13-[_] I Believe that it is Fair to say that God Created all Men and Women to be Bisexuals, like Jesus Christ, himself, who was the Perfect Example of a Man who Greatly Loved other Men and Women, equally. (See the *New Testament* for the Proof.)

14-[_] I Believe that People used to have much more Love and Affection than People have nowadays: beCause their Kind Words and Good Deeds are Proof of it. (See the *Bible* for the Proof.)

15-[_] I Believe that Donald Trumpeter Loves his Family, and his Family also Loves him; but, only beCause they do not really Know him, who has a Despicable Heart, who should never be the President of **"The Divided States of United Lies!" (The so-called "United States of North America" in Disguise!) By The Worldwide People's Revolution!®** Book 058.

16-[_] I Believe that Sodomy is a Major Sin, which is Anal Penetrations with Penises, which is Nasty, Filthy, Stinking, Demeaning, Dehumanizing, Disease-spreading, Humiliating and only Practiced by Ignorant Fools, who have not yet Discovered Frot Sex, who are Looking for HIV-AIDS. ‡

17-[_] I Believe that Donald Trumpeter is not Interested in Frot Sex; but, it is for Sure that he Spiritually and Financially Sodomized tens of thousands of People who Worked for him, beginning with some Polacks from Poland, which was also a Major Sin, who will be Equally as Guilty as Sodomites during the Day of God's Judgment — none of whom will have any Inheritance in the Holy Kingdom of All that is GOOD. †§‡

18-[_] I Believe that Kings and Presidents should be Above the Lewdness that was Displayed by Donald Trumpeter and Bill Adulterous Lying Clinton, whose Hearts were not Right with God. ‡ (See *Matthew 5:28.*)

19-[ ] I Believe that it is now Time for each Man to be the King of his own Swanky Castle, and be Responsible for Raising his own Family, Properly, whereby his Children do not become such Whoremongers as James Bond. ‡

20-[ ] I Believe that all Movies are GOOD, and that none of them ever Influenced anyone to Say nor Do any Evil Thing, nor any Good Thing. †§‡

21-[ ] I Believe that it is now Time to GRADE all Things, and especially those Movies, which should mostly be Avoided by Righteous People, who have Better Things to do. However, if someone Wants to Watch Pornography, for Example, that someone should Visit a Swanky Fortress where it is Legal to Watch it, and no one will be Spying on anyone for doing it, nor making any Records of it, whereby the Privacy of everyone will be Protected. Indeed, People who Live in High-ranking Fortresses may Visit Low-ranking Fortresses at any Time that they Want to, and even go all of the Way Down to HELL; but, People of Low-ranking Fortresses will have to have Special Permission to Visit High-ranking Fortresses, which will Prevent much Corruption among those Fortresses: beCause the Innocent People will not be Exposed to the Lewdness of Low-ranking Fortresses.

D-[ ] **Jil Stiin:** Our National Security depends more on our Righteousness, than on our Security Cameras: because a Nation is most often Destroyed from within it, by the Corrupted People, themselves, who Exclude the Laws of God from their Lives, which Explains many of those Daily Shootings that go on in Chicago, for Example, among Gangs of Outlaws, who were Raised without Respect for their Great Creator God, which they might have, if they had to Grow their own Foods, and make their own Clothes, and get their Minds Off of their Violence. After all, it is a bit Difficult to be Violent while Petting a Kid Goat in your Arms, or Hoeing Weeds around your Flowers. ‡

E-[ ] **Gary Jonsun:** I have to Confess that there is a much Better Way to Live than most of us Americans now Live and Die. However, getting ourselves Transitioned over to a New Lifestyle could Prove to be the Destruction of the Great False Economy, which will Naturally Upset many Greedy Capitalists, who will not Want to Surrender to Reason nor Logic for even one Day.

06-12 [ ] **Moderator:** Our next Important Question is concerning Corporate Crimes — such as the Bursting Housing Bubble Scam, whereby hundreds of millions of People were Bankrupted. What are your Thoughts about such Crimes, and their Appropriate Punishments?

A-[ ] **Hilarious Hillary:** I Propose that all Corporate Criminals should receive Minimum Punishments: because we do not want to Spook Away any more Corporations, since we have already Lost enough Jobs in America. However, in the Cases of the Lying Red Jew Banksters, who created the Bursting Housing Bubble, I believe that it would be Good to Crucify them Upside Down, if they do not make Full Restitutions to the People who were Wronged by them: because they have billions of dollars sitting around doing nothing, which those Poor People could use. †§

B-[_] **Donald Trumpeter:** Well, being a Corporate Criminal, myself, I naturally feel that we should be Compassionate toward Corporate Criminals, and give to them some Tax Breaks: because it was likely a Shortage of Money that Drove them to Commit their Crimes. For Example, I Claim to have Billions of Dollars, and yet I have been sending out E-mail Letters BEGGING my Followers to Contribute 3 to 3,000$ or more to my Election Deception Campaign: because I am Actually a Poor Person, who finds it Difficult to Live on a million dollars per Day. After all, the Property Taxes on the Trump Tower are no less than a million dollars per Year, if you can Believe it — not to Mention all of the other Trump Towers and Golf Courses around the World. Therefore, I have to do a little Conniving to get Out of those Tax Traps. Personally, if I were the President, I would Try to Reward those Corporate Criminals for being able to Survive in such a False Economic System, which has got to be an Invention of Satan, himself: because a Person can go from Riches to Rags in just one Day, which would be Impossible if we all Lived in those **"GLORIOUS Swanky Hotels Castles and Fortresses!" (Beautiful Planned City States for WISE Intelligent Well-Educated People with Common Sense and Good Understanding!) By The Worldwide People's Revolution!®** Book 019.

C-[_] **Our Elected King:** I Propose that we give to those Corporate Criminals 3 Choices, which are as follows:

> 1-[_] Call for and DEMAND **"The Great Worldwide TELEVISED Court HEARING!"** ... or:
>
> 2-[_] Distribute all of your Wealth to the Poor People of the World, and Live in the Abandoned Factories of Detroit, Michigan, or:
>
> 3-[_] Take a Chance that you will not be Boiled in Hot Used Motor Oil when we Hold that Great Meeting of the Most Intelligent Minds!

D-[_] **Jil Stiin:** I Suggest that we pour Molten Gold down their Throats, if they do not Confess all of the Corporate Sins, and do their Best to Promote the Construction of those **"GLORIOUS Swanky Hotels Castles and Fortresses,"** Worldwide, until almost everyone has Moved into them. Otherwise, they should Present at least 3 Great Disadvantages for Righteous People Building them and Living within the Borders of them. †§‡

E-[_] **Gary Jonsun:** I Propose that all Corporations — Criminals or not — should have to Fill Out and File on the Internet **"The Complete SURVEYS of our VALUES,"** whereby we might Learn what their Values are, and whether or not they have our Interests in Mind when they Produce their Capitalist Trash or whatever. ‡

06-13 [_] **Moderator:** Our next Question concerns Health Care, which Costs Americans more than 4 Trillion Dollars per Year — Thanks to Junk Foods, Refined Sugars, Flours, Chemical Poisons, Pollution from Vehicles, Poor Nutrition, Undernourishment, Over-nourishment, Obesity, Smoking, Drug Consumption, Food Poisoning, Accidents, Shootings, Wars, and Various Kinds of EVILS, which would not be the Case within most Swanky Fortresses, which

(It is Time for some Sane Person to get Control of this Insane World!)

would Provide a HIGH Standard of Living with Natural Foods and Drinks. So, what are your Thoughts concerning our Health Care Systems?

A-[_] **Hilarious Hillary:** Well, now that my Mind has been somewhat Enlightened, after Studying: **"Did God or Satan Ordain Medical Doctors??" (Ask Huck Finn and/or Nigger Jim: because neither Tom Sawyer nor Judge Thatcher would Know!) By The Worldwide People's Revolution!®**, Book 022, I have Concluded that our Elected King has the Best Solutions for the Health Care Problems, beginning with a Wholesome Natural Diet on Foods that have been Grown by: **"The LUSCIOUS All-Mineral Organic Method of Gardening!" (HOW to Grow DELICIOUS Satisfying Foods for Potential Kingz and Kweenz in Swanky PALACES!)** Book 021. Indeed, there is no getting around the Fact that we have Broken Natural Dietary Laws, among many other Laws, which have brought about our Long List of Ailments of Mind, Spirit, and Body, which is rather Shameful for the so-called "Greatest Nation on the Earth!"

B-[_] **Donald Trumpeter:** I am the Healthiest Man who has ever ran for the Presidency of **"The Divided States of United Lies,"** which is Proof that I have a Good Diet, and nothing to Repent of, in spite of Weighing at least 50 Pounds too much: because I am just another one of those SLOBS, you might say. However, I do not Object to everyone having Good Wholesome Natural Foods to Eat and Drink, if that is Possible. My Instincts tell me that it is now Impossible: beCause the Skies are Filled with Capitalist Industrial Poisons, including Aluminum, which has been Sprayed into the Upper Atmosphere by Jet Airplanes, which leave what is called ChemTrails, or Chemical Trails, whereby the Aluminum Content in Lakes is as much as 90 Times the EPA's Recommended Amount for Safe Levels of Aluminum. Therefore, just as long as such Capitalist Dung is being Rained Down on our Lands and Gardens and Water Supplies, HOW are we going to Obtain Wholesome Natural Foods? The Sad Part about this Story is the Fact that Medical Doctors already know that Aluminum Causes Alzheimer's Disease, or a Bad Memory, which is WHY the Federal Government Introduced Stainless Steel Pots and Pans to Serve Foods in to the Army, Navy, Marines, and Air Force at least 50 Years ago; but, now they are using Aluminum again: beCause they are Deliberately Attempting to get as much Aluminum into our Diets as Possible, which is WHY Aluminum Beer and Coke Cans are still Legal: beCause they LOVE us. Meanwhile, the CONgress just Sits on their Thumbs and do nothing about it: beCause they are a Part of the Military Industrial Congressional Medical Bankers' Complex, which Requires more and more Sick Degenerated Children and Victims of Capitalism to TREAT with Drugs, whereby the Red Jew Drug Manufacturers have Raked in no less than 20 Trillion Dollars during the past 100 Years, Worldwide. Yes, the Drug Business is America's Number 1 Source of Income for those Rich Lying Red Jews, who Love every Penny of it. Moreover, as if that were not Bad Enough, when People use those Drugs, the Residues are Pissed Out into their Toilets and Urinals, where it Runs into Polluted Rivers, along with many other Toxic Capitalist Chemicals and Poisons, whereby we are all getting Overdosed with Drugs, if we Consume any such Water, even if it has been Treated with other Chemicals and Poisons to supposedly "Clean" it and "Purify" it, which is just a JOKE: beCause the one and only Way that such Water can be Purified, is for it to EVAPORATE, and Ascend Up to Heaven, and come back down as Acid Rains, carrying a Trainload of Toxic Poisons with it: beCause we Earthlings send up no less than 200 Billion Tons of Toxic Poisons, Daily, into our Capitalist Atmosphere! But, not to Worry: beCause we are all going to Heaven when we Die, anyway. Yes, Jesus will Welcome us with Open Arms, and say: "Well Done, you Faithful and Honorable Servants — enter into the Joy of your Supreme Ruler" — to which we will Respond: "O Lord, we knew that you would Forgive us for our Greed: beCause your Mercies Endure Forever, just as MuhamMAD stated in the Holy Koran no less than 4,000 Times: because it is the Truth" — to which he will Reply: "DEPART from me, O you Workers of Iniquities: beCause I never Knew you!" †§‡§§ (See *Matthew 7:23; 25:41; Luke 13:27;* and *Jeremiah 31:36*.)

C-[_] **Our Elected King:** Well, my most Reasonable Solutions for our Health Care Problems are Outlined in several Inspired Books. {See: **"The Gospel According to The Worldwide People's Revolution!®" (The Good News from the Most Modern Perspective!)**, Book 013, plus: **"HOW to Become a HOLY Man!" (40 Good Reasons WHY People Should FAST and PRAY!)**, Book 045, plus: **"The Proper RULES for FASTING!" (The Complete Instruction Manual for True Repentance!)** Book 046.}

D-[_] **Jil Stiin:** I must Confess that our Elected King has it all Figured Out.

E-[_] **Gary Jonsun:** Amen to that.

06-14 [_] **Moderator:** Our next Question concerns Economics. Do any of you Sincerely Believe that our Great False Economy can Endure for another 100 Years?

A-[_] **Hilarious Hillary:** Well, I am Worried for my Granddaughter, who is likely to Inherit a very Mean Miserable World, unless this Generation Wakes Up and Builds those **"GLORIOUS Swanky Hotels Castles and Fortresses!"** After all, we do have Limited Natural Resources to Work with, except for ROCKS, Sand, Gravel, and Limestone for making Cement, which can be made by Solar Power, using Mirrors. However, only some Places are Sunny enough to make it Workable.

B-[_] **Donald Trumpeter:** I am not too Worried about the Future: because it is all going to Work Out Wrong, anyway. Indeed, almost all Human Activities have Proven to be Insane to one Degree or another. For Example, when I was Boy, Football was a Good Game to Play; but, now it has been Discovered that Head Injuries Cause Brain Damage, which makes all such Ball Games Dangerous, if not Deadly. Therefore, we will have to Change our Ways of Living, if we Want a High Standard of Living. Frankly, I Seriously Doubt that our Great False Economy can go on for another 20 Years. However, why Chance it, seeing that the Oceans are RISING, and the Icebergs are MELTING, and the Glaciers are Disappearing all around the World. Perhaps the Earth will FLIP on its Axis, and leave us Stranded at the South Pole! I would not know what is going to Happen; but, it seems to be a very Spooky Time to Live.

C-[_] **Our Elected King:** It was just a few Years ago when Gasoline was 4$ per Gallon, and Rising, while 800,000+ Jobs were being Lost per Month, which Caused a lot of People to Sell their Silver and Gold, which those Lying Red Jews Capitalized on: beCause Gold went up to about 2,000$ per Ounce, from about 400$ per Ounce, and 32$ per Ounce about 50 Years ago, when I should have been Buying all that I could, rather than Wasting Money, Time, and Energy on Construction Projects, whereby I Lost at least 300,000$ worth of Investments, plus 30 Years of Hard Work on a single Farm. Therefore, had I Bought Gold, and Saved it until now, I could have Cashed in with a Good Retirement Plan, whereby I could have Helped myself and many other Poor People; but, there was nothing in the Bible about Buying Gold, and Saving it for Hard Times. I would say that the Great False Economy will CRASH at just any Time, and most People will Suffer for it: beCause of putting their Trust in those Lying Red Jews, who Control the Money Supply.

D-[_] **Jil Stiin:** I am Worried about being Destroyed by Nuclear Weapons, which could End Civilization as we know it. However, the World's Greatest Threat, right now, is Climate Changes. Scientists are most Worried about it.

E-[_] **Gary Jonsun:** I have Learned to not Worry myself about anything. After all, it is Obvious that America is Doomed, sooner or later: beCause of Crossing too many Lines. It is just the Natural Course of Nations, which begin with Poverty, Honesty, Truths and all such Good Things; only to Progress at the Expense of Natural Resources, if they are Available, which, in our Case, just Happened to be Abundant, which brought us into a State of Great PRIDE, as if we had Created all such Natural Resources, ourselves, which has Produced a False Pride, which will Prove to be the Destruction of us, if we do not Repent and Do what is Right for one another and our Naaberz, which will Require some Honesty and Humiliation. Otherwise, we are Doomed, in my Honest Opinion.

06-15 [_] **Moderator:** What do you Think about Whistleblowers? Should they be Prosecuted for Exposing Government Transgressions of our Freedoms; or, should they be Rewarded with **"Beautiful Swanky PALACES"**?

A-[_] **Hilarious Hillary:** Well, in the Case of Edward Snowden, he is still Free; but, not Happy: because he is not Able to Live in **"The Divided States of United Lies!"** Most likely he does not Like those Long Cold Winters in Russia, and neither would I, much less Confinement to a certain Area, which makes him a Prisoner of Sorts. Nevertheless, I do Appreciate what he did for our Sakes, which was Heroic. However, in the Case of Chelsea Manning, she was Sentenced to 35 Years in Prison for doing what was Right, which I would Repeal, if I were the President, and Pardon her for it: because she did it with a Good Conscience, and not with Malicious Intents.

B-[_] **Donald Trumpeter:** I would have had Chelsea Manning Executed, just Yesterday; but, now that I Realize that we were all Brainwashed with Government Propagandist Lies from the Time that we first went to School, I would Reward Chelsea with a Place in a Swanky Palace, and Assign her Accusers to be her Servants, and make the Judge who Sentenced her into a Janitor for Life, who Cleans Toilets and Bathrooms.

C-[_] **Our Elected King:** I would use their Cases for Good Reasons to Establish **"The New RIGHTEOUS One-World Government,"** which would not Need any Whistleblowers: beCause all Meetings of the Minds would be Public, and would be Published to all Nations in all Major Languages: so that nothing is Secret, anymore. Therefore, it would be a Transparent Government with Open Courtrooms.

06-16 [_] **Moderator:** Our so-called Debate has now come to an End. However, it is Possible for us to take up any Important Questions that might be Generated by this Inspired Book for another "Debate" in Future Chapters.

    A-[_] **Hilarious Hillary:** Please wait a minute, O Moderator: because I did not get to make my Final Statements; and neither did the other Candidates.

    B-[_] **Moderator:** Sorry about that. I forgot that you Candidates might want to make Final Statements. After all, I Thought that it has already been Concluded that our Elected King has the Best Solutions for our Massive Problems.

    C-[_] **Donald Trumpeter:** We have not yet Accepted any Questions from the Audience, who might have a thousand or more Important Questions.

    D-[_] **Moderator:** All of their Silly Questions have already been Answered in the Inspired Books of our Elected King. However, those **"GLORIOUS Swanky Hotels Castles and Fortresses"** will Solve nearly all of our Problems. Therefore, when you Think of a Problem, Remember those Fortresses, which Provide a Way for Righteous People to Avoid all such Problems. For Example, how can Drunk Drivers run into you with their Cars, if there are NO Cars within Swanky Fortresses: beCause of Using Electric Elevators and Subway Trains? How can your Daughter get Raped by some Bully, if she is Working beside you at Home, and must do her Courting in the Parlor, if she has a Boyfriend? How can your Children be using Drugs, if there are no Illegal Drugs in your Beautiful Planned City State, which does not have Traffic coming and going like some City of Confusion: because each City is somewhat Self-sufficient and Self-contained: because everyone is Employed at Home or near Home? How could anyone be Cheated Out of their Wages with **"The New RIGHTEOUS One-World Government"** in Charge of all Money and Wages? Indeed, if anyone has Complaints about his or her Wages, they only need to Talk with an Inspecting General of that Good Government, who will be Living within their own Swanky Fortress, doing his own Gardening, and Working in his own Home-craft Workshop: because of having so few Complaints to Attend to, which Complaints will be Recorded by Video Cameras, which may be Presented in a Courtroom for True Justice: beCause there will be NO SECRET MEETINGS in the Swanky Fortress System, nor anything to Hide! Therefore, if someone Wants to Complain to their Elected King or Queen about some Problem, they are Welcome to do it Publically, at some Meeting of the Minds, whereby everyone can Listen and Learn, which is also how Moses and King David Handled all such Complaints, which seemed to have Worked very Well.

    E-[_] **Donald Trumpeter:** So, are you saying that if some Woman stands up at one of my Campaign Speeches to Complain about me Grabbing her in the Crotch, that I am supposed to Respond to such False Accusations, knowing that I am Perfectly Innocent of any Wrongdoings?

    F-[_] **Our Elected King:** If you were Perfectly Innocent of any Wrongdoings, WHY would any Woman be making a Public Disgrace of herself at any Election Deception Campaign, knowing that the Penalty for False Accusations is a Year or more of Hard Labor in a Rock Quarry, depending on the Seriousness of it? Indeed, she can be Thankful

(It is Time for some Sane Person to get Control of this Insane World!)

if her Lying Tongue is not Cut Out for making any such False Accusations. Therefore, it is Extremely Doubtful that anyone is going to be making any False Accusations, if I am in Charge of Things around here — that is, IF I am Elected to be the KING of **"The New RIGHTEOUS One-World Government!" (HOW to Establish a Righteous One-World Government without Going to WAR!) By The Worldwide People's Revolution!® Book 056.**

G-[_] God Speaks: Let him who Speaks, Speak as the Oracles of God, and thus Speak the Truth at all Times and in all Places, and there will be no Problems; but, only IF — only on the CONDITION — that a Righteous Government has been Established, which Deals Justly and Fairly with all of the People, which has Equal Wages for Equal Services, which is made Possible by Constructing those **"GLORIOUS Swanky Hotels Castles and Fortresses"** for everyone in the World, who Joins **"The Swanky Associations of Working Soldiers,"** and goes to WORK, whose Wages will be the Privilege of Living within **"Beautiful Swanky PALACES!" (A New Concept in Living Habits — Swanky Palaces for Poor People, Rich People, Healthy People, Sick People, Sane People, and Insane People!)** Yes, whomever does his or her Best to Help Build all such Palaces, should Inherit them, even if they are Presently Insane: beCause I know HOW to Heal them by Means of Fasting and Praying! Yes, they must come to me in the Name of Jesus Christ, their Anointed Savior, and thus Confess ALL of their Sins, and thus take up Fasting and Praying, whereby they will be Healed, even if they are Totally INSANE: beCause the Elders of the Churches must also Fast and Pray with them, until they are Healed, according to **"The Proper RULES for FASTING!" (The Complete Instruction Manual for True Repentance!)**, Book 046, which I have Inspired for your Salvation. Therefore, if anyone Disagrees to Work with **"The Swanky Associations of Working Soldiers,"** such a Person only needs to be LEFT ALONE, and SHUNNED by the People who Agree to Work Together, whereby such a Person will come to his or her Right Senses after getting Hungry Enough, whereby he or she will Willingly Submit to Reason and Logic! Yes, it is only Reasonable that everyone should be Happy to Live within their own **"Beautiful Swanky PALACES!"** Therefore, I Command you People to Establish **"The New RIGHTEOUS One-World Government,"** and to Build **"The Great World TEMPLE of PEACE,"** in Jerusalem, for the Headquarters of that Good Government, whereby each Nation can Elect Righteous MEN to Govern them, who will Represent them, who will do what is RIIT for all of them, who will Provide a Way for all of them to become Moderately RICH, without Telling any Lies, nor Selling any Trash! And all of the Righteous People will say a Hearty, "AMEN — so let it be Done!"

H-[_] Moderator: So, is there anyone who Objects to that Master Plan? If so, you must Present your Objections at: **"The Great Worldwide TELEVISED Court HEARING,"** which will Temporarily be Held in Saint Peter's Basilica, in the Vatican, if the Pope of Rome does not Object to it. After all, he is a Man of Peace, who Sincerely Believes in Justice for ALL Peoples, Worldwide. Therefore, unless he has become a Son of Satan, he should Rejoice with that Great Opportunity to get True Justice for ALL Peoples.

I-[_] An Innocent Lamb of God Speaks: Now I Know WHO can be Trusted — it is the Person who DEMANDS **"The Great Worldwide TELEVISED Court HEARING!" (That Great Meeting of the Most Intelligent Minds!) By The Worldwide People's**

Revolution!® Book 041. Indeed, all other People, who Object to that Plan are Anti-Christs: beCause God also Demands it.

J-[ ] True Justice will never be Served, until the Whole Truth is Revealed to the Masses of People about all Important Subjects, which is WHY that I have Checked the above Box with an X, with Red Ink, and Signed my Name here:

K-[ ] Would you Kindly Explain to us just HOW we Tax Slaves are going to FORCE almost everyone in the World to Study this Inspired Book, and to make their own Check Marks with whatever Statements that they Agree with: so that they might be Held Accountable as Electors, who have a Right to VOTE for anyone: beCause of Qualifying?

L-[ ] Lots of Laughs! It cannot be Done.

M-[ ] People will Say and Do just about anything for more MONEY. Therefore, you should Offer to Buy the Book for whomever cannot Afford it, and to Pay them for Reading it: so that they will be Convicted by the Great Truths within it, whereby they will be Willing to do the same Good Deed for their Poor Lost Confused Friends, Relatives, and Naaberz. Indeed, it must become like a Contagious Disease, which Spreads like Wild Fires throughout the Dry Forest, which cannot be Quenched by any Means, until it has Accomplished its Goal, which is Worldwide Peace and True Prosperity!

N-[ ] Not everyone is going to Buy into that Plan, even though it is Guaranteed to WORK: beCause 99% or more of the People are Willing to do Good Things for more Money, including Selling all of the Inspired Books by **The Worldwide People's Revolution!®**

O-[ ] Are there no OPTIONS? Must we Establish a RIGHTEOUS One-World Government, just to Build those **"GLORIOUS Swanky Hotels Castles and Fortresses!"**? Can we not Build them by Investing our own Moneys in them?

P-[ ] All of the Money of all of People in the World, would not PAY for even ONE of those Glorious Fortresses, if it were a hundred Miles in Diameter. Moreover, just a Small Swanky Fortress might Cost a Trillion Dollars. ‡

Q-[ ] The Great Question is this: **"What is WRong with us Tax Slaves Claiming our own Mountains of Rocks, Rivers of Water, Deserts of Sand, and whatever Natural Resources that are Needed for the Construction of those Glorious Fortresses?"** Indeed, we can make this next Year a Great Year of JUBILEE, whereby all of the Natural Resources are Returned to the Masses of People, Worldwide, whereby everyone can Rejoice with their Riches, which they must then Use WISELY for the Construction of those **"Beautiful Swanky PALACES!" (A New Concept in Living Habits — Swanky Palaces for Poor People!) By The Worldwide People's Revolution!®** Book 066. After all, there are more than 5,000 Good Reasons and Great Advantages for doing that! ‡

R-[ ] I am Ready to go to WORK. Therefore, WHERE do I Sign Up?

(It is Time for some Sane Person to get Control of this Insane World!)

S-[_] You can Sign Up just as soon as we Tax Slaves, Interest Slaves, Insurance Slaves, and Work Slaves DEMAND: **"The Great Worldwide TELEVISED Court HEARING,"** whereby we can Establish **"The New RIGHTEOUS One-World Government,"** whereby we can all go to WORK for those Reasonable Solutions!

T-[_] I Prefer to Vote for a Powerless President, like Donald Trumpeter, or Hilarious Clinton: beCause I Love those Election Deceptions, which give to me Erectile Dysfunctionus Maximus. †§

U-[_] We Understand that you are Crazy, and need to do some Fasting and Praying.

V-[_] I am a Victim of Capitalism, which has me Greatly Confused, whereby I have no Idea what to Think, much less, what to DO.

W-[_] Well, when you get Drafted into some Murderous Army of Bloody Warriors, you will not have any Freedom to Say nor Do anything. Indeed, you will be like the Woman who Telephoned the *Washington Journal,* saying that if she got into an Accident, all she was Permitted to Say was that she was Working for the CIA (Central Intelligence Agency): because, if she said any more than that, she would be facing a 10,000$ Fine and as much as 10 Years in Prison! Yes, she Lives in "the freest nation on the earth," according to SINator Blabbermouth the Third, whereby she has Forfeited ALL of her Civil Rights, beginning with Freedom of Speech! Nevertheless, she Sincerely Believes that it is her DUTY to Vote for one of 2 or 3 or more Right/WRong Rong/Riit Political Parties, none of which have any Reasonable Solutions for anything!

X-[_] X-amount of People would say that our Elected King also has no Reasonable Solutions for anything: beCause it is not Reasonable that we should have to Build any of those **"GLORIOUS Swanky Hotels Castles and Fortresses,"** beCAUSE they would Cost too much — as if Printing Presses were not Able to Print enough Money for Hiring such Work to be Done, even if all of that Money is TRASHED after those **"Beautiful Swanky PALACES"** have been Finished, and everyone is Living within them, in Peace!

Y-[_] I am Yearning for the Great Year of JUBILEE, when all Debts are Forgiven, and the Masses of People get to Hear the Whole Truth at: **"The Great Worldwide TELEVISED Court HEARING!"** Yes, that will be a Time of Great Rejoicing, when the Whole Truth is Discovered about all Important Subjects! Just THINK about that. Meditate on it. Talk about it with your Friends, Relatives, and Naaberz. STUDY it.

Z-[_] The Great ZEAL of **The Worldwide People's Revolution!®** will make it Possible!

— Chapter 07 —

Let the Trumpets Sound!

07-01 [_] Now, if you have Studied the Previous Chapters, you have likely come to the same Happy Conclusion that I have come to — that there is Great Hope for Mankind, and even for the Lowliest of People, unto the Utmost Bounds of the Earth — Thanks to Modern Means of Communications, which make it Possible for Good News and Bad News to be Quickly Published around the World. Moreover, in this Case, the Good News is OVERWHELMING: beCause, until now, there was no Way for almost everyone to become Moderately Rich in all Ways: because no one Presented any Way to DO it; but, now our Elected King has come to the Rescue!

07-02 [_] O Doctor Edison, does **The Worldwide People's Revolution!®** not know that your Elected King is Described in the *Bible* as the *Anti-Christ?* Indeed, all of the World will Wander after the BEAST from Angel Ridge, King's Mountain, Kentucky: beCause of being Deceived by him! †§‡

07-03 [_] Well, I must Inform you, and Kindly so, that YOU have also been Greatly Deceived by a Misunderstanding of the *Scriptures:* beCause our Elected King is anything other than an Anti-Christ BEAST, as you call him, which is Referring to a Great FALSE Government, which is otherwise known as: **"The Divided States of United Lies!" (The so-called "United States of North America" in Disguise!)** Yes, it is Referring to a Beastly GOVERNMENT, which Appears like an Innocent Lamb with Freedom, Liberty, and Justice for ALL, while making Tax Slaves, Interest Slaves, Insurance Slaves, Drug Slaves, Childcare Slaves, Sex Slaves, and Work SLAVES of the Masses of People, including YOURSELF, O FOOL! However, you would have to be Perfectly HONEST, in Order to Confess it, which you are Obviously NOT Willing to be: beCause you Vainly Imagine that you are FREE, in spite of being nothing but a SLAVE! Yes, it can easily be Proven in a Courtroom; but, you are not at all Interested in such Trials: beCause you are the DECEIVED Person, who Actually Sincerely Believes the Propagandist LIES of the Anti-Christ FALSE Federal Government, which now Rules Over you like a BEAST, which has Total Control Over you! Indeed, *"Who can make War against the Beast,"* now that it has Total Control? In Fact, WHO can even get our Elected King's Name on any Election Ballot in **"The Divided States of United Lies!"**?

07-04 [_] O Doctor Edison, you are your Elected King's Chief Editor, and yet you Confess that you are Unable to get his Name on any Election Ballot, which is Proof that his Master Plan must be WRong, or Unworkable. After all, if it were any Good, the Masses of People would be Glomming onto it, as Festus of Gunsmoke Fame might say.

07-05 [_] Once again, you are WRong: beCause the Masses of People have never even Heard of our Elected King's Master Plan, much less have Endless Conversations about it on TV and Radio Talk Shows: beCause of several Reasons; but, mostly beCause of IGNORANCE! Indeed, most of those Ignorant People do not even Watch the Evening News Reports, whereby they are Ignorant about our Massive Problems. However, when the House Fires are Consuming their own

Houses, or the Tornadoes have just Blown their Houses AWAY, some of them do give to it SOME Thoughts; but, no one Enlightens their Minds about what should be Done to PREVENT all such Disasters: beCause it is Illegal in **"The Divided States of United Lies"** to Build a Fireproof, Mouse-proof, Hail-proof, Rot-proof, Paint-proof, Tornado-proof, Hurricane-proof, Earthquake-proof, Flood-proof, Insurance-proof, Self-air-conditioned HOUSE — that is, within any City of Confusion! Indeed, there are a few Remote Places in "Backward" Counties, where it might be Legal, whereby almost no one could SEE such a House; but, the Chief Objection is that NO BANK WILL LOAN ANY MONEY FOR BUILDING SUCH A GOOD HOUSE! Yes, you could call it a Bankers' Conspiracy against the American Tax Slaves, Interest Slaves, Insurance Slaves, Debt Slaves, and Work Slaves: beCause those Friendly Bankers collect TRILLIONS of Dollars from the Ignorant FOOLS who Sincerely Believe that they are FREE, Healthy, and HAPPY! But, in Reality, they are POOR, Wretched and MISERABLE, just as Jesus Christ stated in *Revelation 3!* Therefore, until those Masses of Ignorant Fools WAKE UP and come to their Riit Senses, there is little Hope for them to be Saved from their Troubles.

07-06 [_] O Doctor Edison, I must Confess that you do Present some STRONG and Reasonable Arguments in Favor of your Elected King. Indeed, all of the Arguments seem to be in his Favor. Therefore, WHY has his Tale of Truths not become POPULAR, by now?

07-07 [_] Well, the Main Reason that his Truths have not become Popular, is beCAUSE most Americans do not like to READ. Besides that, they are Distracted by Television Nonsense, Comedies, Sports, Work, the Internet, Eating, Drinking, Joking, Government Propaganda, Election Deceptions, and all such Foolish Things. In Fact, not even the Preachers nor Teachers have TIME to Study all such Inspired Books as this, they say: beCause they have so many other Important Things to Say and Do. Therefore, it is up to the Readers to Draw Attention to **The Worldwide People's Revolution!®** Indeed, they must take Action to make it a BIG Issue; but, only IF they Agree that it would be GOOD for most People to be Living in those **"GLORIOUS Swanky Hotels Castles and Fortresses,"** which are Designed for LIVING, which have ZERO Taxes, Insurance Bills, Heating and Cooling Bills, Insecticides, Herbicides, Chemical Fertilizers, Drugs, Drug Addicts, Drug Pushers, Criminals, Mass Murders, Terrorist Attacks, Car Bombs, Cars, Vans, Pickups, Trucks, Tractors, Motorcycles, Lawnmowers, Chainsaws, Weed-eaters, Buses, Motorboats, Airplanes, nor any other Stinking Noisy ABOMINATIONS! Indeed, none of those Evil Things are Needed for True Prosperity. For Example, Sheeps and Cows can Graze the Grasses under Fruit and Nut Trees, while Workhorses and Oxens can be used Wisely for Generating Electricity when the Wind is not Blowing, and the Water is not Running, and when there are no Fields to be Plowed, Disked, Harrowed, Planted, Cultivated, nor Harvested: beCause that is WHY God Created those Beasts, to Assist us in a Righteous Way, whose Dung makes Perfect Fertilizers for those Luscious All-Mineral Organic Gardens, after being Processed Properly in Methane Digesters, which Produce Gases for Cook Stoves, which should be Used Wisely for Canning Survival Foods: beCause there is no Guarantee from God nor Government that it will always go on Raining!

07-08 [_] O Doctor Edison, did it ever Cross your Weak Mind that most Americans are not Interested in Reverting Back to the 14th Century!? Indeed, we LOVE our Greasy Cars, Noisy Lawnmowers, Polluting Airplanes, Noisy Helicopters, Motorcycles, Garden Tillers, Chainsaws, and all such GOOD Useful Tools, which Jesus Christ and Saint Peter would also LOVE: because our Way of Life is Far Superior to their Way of DEATH, which Produced Billions of Poor

People, who Died with all Kinds of Sicknesses and Diseases, even if they did not Die in Car Accidents, Airplane Crashes, and Mismanaged Medical Treatments, whereby a quarter of a Million Americans are Murdered each Year — all for the Lack of the Tree of Life in the Garden of Eden. †§‡§§

07-09 [_] Well, did it ever Cross your Weak Mind that if all People had been Living Exactly like Present-day Americans during the past 1,000 Years, there would not be one Drop of Gas for you to Burn in your Stinking Noisy Lawnmower, nor one Drop of Motor Oil for your Greasy Car, nor even a Bucket of Coal left to Burn for making your ElecTrickery: beCause it would have all been Used Up by now, O Ostrich? Moreover, if we Insist on Driving on this Highway to Hell, the Great Great Grandchildren will be Cursing us for our Selfishness and GREED, who will have to Submit to **"The Swanky Sword of Divine Truths,"** anyway, or else make themselves EXTINCT! †‡

07-10 [_] O Doctor Edison, I find it most Amazing that anyone on this Earth would Object to Living within those **"Beautiful Swanky PALACES!" (A New Concept in Living Habits — Swanky Palaces for Poor People!) By The Worldwide People's Revolution!®** Book 066.

07-11 [_] Trust me, no Sane Person would Object to it; but, X-amount of Ignorant Fools will Naturally Persuade themselves to Believe that those Swanky Palaces will somehow DESTROY the World! Yes, the Environmentalists will no doubt be coming Out of their Closets, saying that Swanky Fortresses will RUIN the Mountains! — as if there were a Shortage or ROCKS in this World of Wonders! Indeed, at the Expense of the Environment, they should take a Chartered Airplane Ride from Alaska to Chili, with High-definition Cameras on both Sides of the Plane, for taking Movie Pictures of the Scenery: so as to Discover just how MANY Rocks there might be, which Stretch Out "Endlessly" in all Directions, just on these Continents, not to Mention Europe, Asia, and Africa, which have more Mountains of Rocks than North, Central and South America! Nevertheless, I will Confess that most of the Rocks will be Difficult to Move around, which will Require a LOT of Energy, and especially if those Rocks are Gathered from Remote Places in those Mountains, which do not even have Railroad Tracks running to them, which will be a Major Construction Project, itself, even if the Trains are all Electric. Indeed, it is the Inaccessibility of those Mountains of Rocks that have thus far Protected them from Capitalist Exploiters, who have known of their Existence, all along; but, how could they Afford to get them?

07-12 [_] O Doctor Samuel Walker Edison, if we do not Act Wisely, we are likely to Waste a LOT of Expensive Fuel in an Attempt to Harvest those Mountains of Rocks for Building those **"GLORIOUS Swanky Hotels Castles and Fortresses,"** which will Require a lot more Rocks than you might Imagine, if the Solid Stone Walls are 10 to 20 feet THICK! †‡

07-13 [_] Well, there are lots of Rubble Rocks, Sand, and Clay, which can be used to fill in the Spaces between Solid Stone Walls, which will be the Bulk of the Rocks that will be used: beCause of those Wide Spaces, which will Function as Heat Banks and Cold Banks for Stabilizing the Temperatures throughout the Cities, while also making them Bomb-resistant and Tornado-proof. Concrete Tunnels may also be run throughout those Spaces for Plumbing Pipes, Special Lighting Systems, Music Box Connections, Electric-wire Conduits, Secret Passageways, and Bunkers for Defense and State Security. ‡

(It is Time for some Sane Person to get Control of this Insane World!)

— Chapter 08 —

Mudslinging Election Campaigns are Coming to an End!

08-01 [_] If you have Listened to Election Campaigns during the past 20 Years or so, you have no doubt Noticed that there is a LOT of Mudslinging at the Opponents, whereby they make both Parties and perhaps all Parties Appear to be Criminals, Sex Abusers, or whatever — as was also the Case between Hilarious Hillary Clinton and Donald James Trumpeter, which was rather Disgraceful for Potential Presidents to engage in all such Abusive Talk, which only Caused all Parties to be Turned Off by such Candidates, whereby the Electors only Voted for what they perceived to be "the lesser of the 2 evils," or the least likely to get a Nuclear War going, or the most likely to Boost the Great False Economy, or to "bring jobs back home," as if the Chinese and Mexican Peoples did not also Need Jobs, and GOOD Respectable Jobs with Decent Wages. Personally, I am the Biggest Promoter of Respectable Safe Jobs with Fair Swanky Wages for everyone, Worldwide. Indeed, no one else in the Whole World even comes Close to Competing with me for Eternal Jobs for everyone: beCause my Economic Plan is Based on True Prosperity, which Begins with Providing Secure Self-air-conditioned Houses for everyone, Worldwide, which also have Paint-proof Polished Marble Walls, Polished Granite Floors, Agate Windows, Gold Trimmings, Well-made Tools to Work with, Home-craft Workshops to Work in, Large Swanky Cisterns for Water Storage for every Household, Trillions of Fruit and Nut Trees, Luscious All-Mineral Organic Gardens, Walk-in Root Cellars / Coolers / Freezers, Spacious Kitchens, Comfortable Bedrooms with Spacious Bathrooms, and large Living Rooms with Wide-screen Flat TV's — not to mention Community Churches, Cathedrals, Mosques, Synagogues, Temples, Auditoriums, Entertainment Centers, Gymnasiums, Theaters, Concert Halls, Tennis Courts, Indoors Swimming Pools, Bowling Alleys, and whatever the People are Willing and Able to Work for, FREE of Charges, FREE of all Taxes, FREE of Loans and Interest on Loans, FREE of Insurance Bills, FREE of all Debts, and with FREE Education for everyone: beCause of United Effort and Cooperation. However, if anyone Disagrees with my Master Plan, PLEASE STAND UP and Explain yourself!

> A-[_] I Agree that you do have a Utopian Dream that I Love, O Elected King; but, getting these People to VOTE for it is another Subject.
>
> B-[_] I Believe that it is all Possible, and even Practical, if everyone Cooperates; but, X-amount of Nations are likely to Rebel against the Idea, on Account of making Old Tourist Sites of little or no Interest to any Visitors, which are now a Major Source of Income. ‡
>
> C-[_] I Confess that it would be the Best Plan ever put into Practice, if some Wicked Lying Red Jews did not end up getting Control of **"The New RIGHTEOUS One-World Government!"**
>
> D-[_] DUMBmocracy must Learn to Speak Up for itself, and thus DEMAND: **"The Great Worldwide TELEVISED Court HEARING,"** whereby those Lying Red Jews can be DEHORNED and CASTRATED, and Satan Locked Up in his Prison for at least a

thousand Years: beCause of Exposing all of his Lies, and Stripping him of his Powers. Indeed, that will be a Time of Great Rejoicing for the Righteous Ones.

E-[_] Educated People know that Satan is far too Tricky and Deceiving to be Defeated by DUMBmocracy. Indeed, he and his Servants will no doubt be Inventing all Kinds of Lies for Speaking Evil of our Elected King, who Eats Children for Supper, and Drinks the Blood of his Victims, and Sucks on Penises in Washington, and Licks Up the Spit of Puppet Politicians, and Pisses on the Head of the Pope of Rome, and Dungs on the Heads of Women Liberators, and Mocks the National Anthem, and Burns the American Rag, and Whitewashes the White House with the Blood of Veterans, and Walks on the Train of the Queen of England: beCause of being the Lowest and Basest of Men who were ever Born! Yes, Lying Witnesses will Surely Appear from the Woodwork, to Speak EVIL of our Elected King: beCause of ENVY! Yes, they will Envy him for all Kinds of Reasons; but, mostly beCause they did not Think of his Economic System, which Provides True Justice for ALL Peoples. †§‡§§

F-[_] I Fail to Understand WHY anyone would Object to our Elected King's Economic Plan: beCause, if some Capitalist Wants to, he or she is Welcome to Produce and Sell whatever he or she can Invent, whereby he or she could get Excessively RICH, if that were any Good. After all, what would such a Person Spend his or her Money on, seeing that Cars will become Obsolete, except for perhaps a few Elected Cars for Elected Officials to Travel around in on Abandoned Highways, which will be Growing Up to Weeds, Briars, and Thorn Trees!? †§‡§§

G-[_] God Knows that it will be Good for almost all People to become Moderately RICH, whereby no one will be Envying Rich People, nor Seeking any of their Vain Riches: beCause they will become Healthy, whereby they will have the True Wealth, which will make those Vain Toys Obsolete. Yes, go tell it on the Mountains, and in every Valley, that Jesus Christ is the SUPREME Ruler of the RIGHTEOUS Ones!

H-[_] HUMBUG! Jesus Christ is Dead and Gone, even though Humble Honest People still Profess to Believe in him: beCause no one Measures Up to his Goodness and Purity of Character: beCause he is another Jewish MYTH, just like the Remainder of that Red Jew Bible, which is more Hilarious than Hillary! †§‡§§

I-[_] Innocent People Love our Elected King's Master Plan: beCause he Proposes that we all Live SIMPLE Uncomplicated Lives. {See: **"Has your Life become Extremely Complicated?" (HOW to Live a SIMPLE Life!) By The Worldwide People's Revolution!®** Book 068.

J-[_] Justice Demands that all Poor People should be given a Chance to make themselves Moderately Rich, even if they Choose to do otherwise, which they are Welcome to VOTE for: beCause that is what DEMON-ocracy is Good for. †§‡§§

K-[_] King Jesus will not have any Election Deceptions: because he will simply Appoint whomever he Chooses to Govern us, Properly.

(It is Time for some Sane Person to get Control of this Insane World!)

L-[_] Lots of Laughs! Those same Silly Ignorant Demon-possessed People could simply Vote for the Construction of those **"GLORIOUS Swanky Hotels Castles and Fortresses,"** by Rich People, like Donald Trumpeter and Bill Computer Software Gates, Incorporated, who could Hire the Military to do the Work at Minimum Wages; and then when all of those **"Beautiful Swanky PALACES"** are Finished, those Poor People could Move into them, and make those Rich People into their SLAVES — that is, IF there were any Power in DUMBmocracy! But, there AIN'T. †§‡§§

M-[_] Money is no longer a Problem: beCause we have the New RIGHTEOUS One-World GovernMINT for Handling that Problem. {See: **"The CONSTITUTION for the New RIGHTEOUS One-World GovernMINT!"** (HOW all Peoples can get True Justice, and Celebrate the Great Year of JUBILEE!) By The Worldwide People's Revolution!® Book 016.} Yes, that is the whole Purpose for Building **"The Great World TEMPLE of PEACE!"** (The Glory of Jerusalem Arises Again!), which will be the Headquarters for: **"The New RIGHTEOUS One-World Government!"** (HOW to Establish a Righteous One-World Government without Going to WAR!) By The Worldwide People's Revolution!® Book 056.

N-[_] I will Vomit, if I Hear those NASTY Words one more Time! {See: **"The New MAGNIFIED Version of ISAIAH in Plain English!"** (The Understandable Version of the Book of Isaiah!), Book 044, plus: **"The New MAGNIFIED Version of The Book of MOORMUN!"** (The Story of the White and Dark Indians in the Americas!) By The Worldwide People's Revolution!®, Book 040, which do not contain any Advertisements for other Books, except in very Rare Cases, where it is Appropriate.}

O-[_] It is my Honest Opinion that all of the Enlightening Books of our Elected King are Inspired by the Omnipotent, Omnipresent and Omniscient GOD, who Knows everything, except HOW to get these Inspired Words of Provable Truths into the Minds and Hearts of all Good People! †§‡

P-[_] There are NO Good People: beCause, *"all have Sinned and Fallen far Short of the Glory of the Gods,"* even as the *Scriptures* Reveal. Therefore, stop Looking for Perfect People, and do your ever-loving Best to make it Possible for most People to become Good People, by DEMANDING **"The Great Worldwide TELEVISED Court HEARING,"** whereby the Whole Truth about all Important Subjects might be Discovered and Published, Worldwide! †§‡

Q-[_] The Great Question is this: **"Does any Potential President, King, Prime Minister, or other Leader on this Earth, present a Better Master Plan than our Elected King has Presented in Plain English, who is the Author of more than 350 Inspired Books, which Speak to our Souls?"** I Think NOT!

R-[_] Righteous People do not BOAST about their Great Achievements. Therefore, your Elected King is a Religious Hypocrite!

S-[_] Satan has Greatly Deceived you: beCause Doctor Sam made that Statement — NOT our Elected King. Indeed, you seem to have Forgotten that anyone and everyone is

Welcome to make Statements within our Elected King's Inspired Books, which are Equally as Enlightening as anything that one might Discover in the *Scriptures,* if not more Enlightening: beCause all Truths are Inspired by the GODS. †§‡

T-[_] I will be Happy to Testify in any Courtroom in Favor of our Elected King, who is the Most Righteous Man among us, who does not have a Selfish Greedy Bone in his entire Body, who has Sacrificed almost everything to Try to Save us from our Capitalist Madness, which has Produced so many Terrorists and Tyrants with Long Tally Whackers and Red Tongues, which are Covered with Innocent Blood from Raping the Children, who will be Burdened with Endless DEBTS — Thanks to the God of Confusion, who did not make the Truth Crystal Clear in that Unholy Mutilated Bible, which should be put on Trial at: **"The Great Worldwide TELEVISED Court HEARING,"** so as to Prove HOW this World got so Messed Up by Teat-sucking Trumpeters, if you know what I Mean. Isaiah would know. †§‡§§

U-[_] I Understand all of the Words, and even Relate with some of them; but, I do not Understand WHY you are Mudslinging against those Trumpeters of the World, who may have LOUD Mouths, and Absurd Ideas; but, at least they are Able to get our Attention, if not our Votes. †§‡

V-[_] I will Vote for the most Righteous Person among us, if he can be Discovered. For Sure, it is NOT Hilarious Hillary, nor Donald Trumpeter, who have not Filled Out nor Filed on the Internet **"The Complete SURVEYS of our VALUES!"** (SURVEYS of **Religious Spiritual Political Governmental Sexual Social Moral Economic Business Labor Habitual and Miscellaneous VALUES!**), whereby we might Determine with Reason and Logic **"WHO QUALIFIES to Rule Over US!"** {See www.Amazon.com for: **"LIGHTNING Versus the Lightning Bug!"** (HOW almost Everyone can become Moderately RICH, without Telling Any Lies nor Selling Any Trash!), which contains 2 very Important Documents, called: **"The New MAGNIFIED Version of the Ten Commandments in Plain English,"** and: **"WHO QUALIFIES to Rule Over US?"** Yes, those Documents are most Enlightening to the Mind of Greater Faith, even though there are many other Inspired Pieces of Literature that everyone should Study — such as *The Declaration of Interdependence,* which can be found in: **"The Low Court of Supreme Injustices is Brought to Trial!" (The Worldwide People's Revolution!® Butts Heads with the United States Supreme Court, with or without their Black Robes of Hypocrisies and Lies!)**, Book 011, which makes President Thomas Jefferson look like a Pumpkinhead, when Compared with our Elected King!}

W-[_] I am Worried that your Elected King might be Worshiped as some GOD, when he is just a Warmongering Son of Satan, who Intends to Divide all of the Nations with **"The Swanky Sword of Divine Truths,"** whereby he will Split their Heads WIDE OPEN, if they do not Humbly Submit, and Willfully Obey the Commandment of God to Build those **"GLORIOUS Swanky Hotels Castles and Fortresses!"** (Beautiful Planned City States for WISE Intelligent Well-Educated People with Common Sense and Good Understanding!) By The Worldwide People's Revolution!® Book 019.

X-[_] X-amount of People would like to Assassinate our Elected King: beCause of him Disrupting their Capitalist Money Games, which they have been Enjoying at the Expense of the Tax Slaves, Interest Slaves, Insurance Slaves, Drug Slaves, Childcare Slaves, and Work Slaves, who have no Idea what it Means to be FREE with a Capital F, much less Free from all Sins, Internal Obstructions of Filth and Poisons and Accumulations of Capitalist GARBAGE, whereby their Minds and Bodies are Tormented both Day and Night: beCause of being Ignorant FOOLS! {See: **"The Gospel According to The Worldwide People's Revolution!®" (The Good News from the Most Modern Perspective!)**, Book 013, which contains a very Special Chapter 06, which is even Better than: **"The UGLY Scarred Dishonest Face of Poor Old Miserable UNCLE SAM!" (A Memorial Day Legacy!) By The Worldwide People's Revolution!®** Book 054.}

Y-[_] And here I was Thinking, just Yesterday, that I had Discovered the Best Book in the World, which is THIS Book! However, now I am Learning that this is only a Mediocre Book, when it comes to Inspired Rivers of Living Waters, which Flow Out of the Heart of our Elected King! Yes, Jesus said, *"He who Believes on me with a Capital B, even as the Scriptures have it Recorded, Out of the Belly of his Mind shall Flow Rivers of Living Water, which will Quench the Thirst of every Hungering Soul for the Pure Truths, which alone can Satisfy the Belly of the Mind!"* — NMV of John 7:38.

Z-[_] The Zeal of **The Worldwide People's Revolution!®** will make it a Reality! Therefore, Sound the Trumpets unto the Ends of the Earth, and Proclaim LIBERTY throughout all of the Lands, unto all of the People, Worldwide: beCause it is now Time for the Great Wedding of the Most Humble Honest Nations, who will Celebrate the Great Year of JUBILEE!

08-02 [_] O Elected King, I have no Idea HOW any Words could get Better than those Words above: because they bring Tears to my Eyes, and Refreshments to my Soul! After all, we have Surely Suffered Long Enough, and are now Ready for a REAL Leader, like YOU! †‡

08-03 [_] Well, I Appreciate your Willingness to Join Forces with me and **The Worldwide People's Revolution!®** However, without some Drastic and Dramatic ACTION on the Part of my Readers, nothing Positive will Happen. Therefore, I now Invite any Good Readers to make DVD Recordings of **The Introduction** to this Inspired Book, and in as many Voices as Possible: so as to Confound the Foxes and Snakes in the District of Criminals, in Washington, and especially the Criminals on Wall Street, in New Yuck City, who will be out to Hunt me Down and Murder me for all such Great Truths, which Threaten to put them Out of Business! Indeed, the more Voices there are, the more they will be Confounded, which can all be Recorded and Copyrighted by **The Worldwide People's Revolution!®** Ask Hollywood for some Help.

08-04 [_] O Elected King, I would call that Plan the Ultimate Mudslinging Campaign, which will be Aimed at the Faces of those Lying Red Jews, who will have to Eventually Surrender to **"The Swanky Sword of Divine Truths!" (The Most Powerful Weapon in the Whole World!) By The Worldwide People's Revolution!®** Book 067.

08-05 [_] Well, it is just a Matter of Time, and the Sword of Truths will WIN this Great Battle between Good and Evil — that is, IF anyone is Brave Enough to USE IT!

08-06 [_] O Elected King, I Promise to take up my own Sword of Truths, and thus Promote your Inspired Books as much as I can, by Pretending to Contradict you, and Prove you to be Rong. Yes, I will Try to make Fun of you, and thus Draw some Attention to you, being like the Devil's Adversary, you might say. After all, there is more than one Way to Skin a Cat, as the Saying goes. Therefore, I will publish a book that does not capitalize the important words, as you have done, whereby such a book will be accepted by the ignorant general public, who will think of me as their hero; but, not with a capital H by any means: because, deep down inside, they will Know that you are the Real Hero, who has taken on the Establishment with **"The Swanky Sword of Divine Truths!"** Therefore, I must be very subtle, even as subtle as a snake, and pretend that I am your enemy, even though I will secretly support you and promote your Inspired Books. †§‡

08-07 [_] Well, I was Hoping that the Secretary General of the United Nations would do that for me, since he is a Man of Peace, and Lover of Truths. Indeed, the Pope of Rome might also do that for me, as well as the Billy Graham Evangelistic Association of Mockingbirds, and the Worldwide Church of God, who now call themselves in some other Name, just to Distinguish themselves from the Seventh-day Adventists, who might find it Interesting to Learn that the True Church will Escape *"on the Wings of a Great Eagle,"* as *the Book of Revelation* puts it. {See: **"The Secret City of the Great King!" (HOW the True Church will Escape from the Great Tribulation!) By The Worldwide People's Revolution!®** Book 042.

08-08 [_] O Elected King, I must Confess that I have never Discovered any Literature that is more Fascinating than your Literature; but, that is only beCause I am a Religious Person. Therefore, I am now Wondering just how Fascinating your Literature might seem to be to People who are NOT Religious, who have been Overcome by Television Soap Operas, Comedies, Sitcoms, Sports, Video Games, Tweeting Nonsense, and all such Silly Things?

08-09 [_] Well, do you Sincerely Think that any of those Silly People are Worthy to Escape from the Great Tribulation? Indeed, their Minds and Bodies must be Purified and Refined, which is the Purpose for that Great Tribulation. Therefore, do not Think that it is Strange if most People Reject whatever I have to Teach: because they are hardly Qualified to Enter into the Holy Kingdom of All that is GOOD, much less Reign as Kings and Priests with Jesus Christ. (See *Revelation 5:10 and 20:6.*)

08-10 [_] Okay, I have to Agree with you, O Elected King — they are Certainly not Worthy of any Positions in the Government of God. However, there is a Way for them to make themselves Worthy, if they Study: **"HOW to Become a HOLY Man!" (40 Good Reasons WHY People Should FAST and PRAY!), Book 045, plus: "The Proper RULES for FASTING!" (The Complete Instruction Manual for True Repentance!) By The Worldwide People's Revolution!®** Book 046.

(It is Time for some Sane Person to get Control of this Insane World!)

— Chapter 09 —

Selected Kings Versus Powerless Presidents!

09-01 [_] Now, it is often said, in one Way or another, in **"The Divided States of United Lies,"** that we have Elected Presidents, who are NOT Kings nor Dictators, who might have Powers to Change Things in a Positive Way. However, I Maintain that a Powerless President is no Better than a Red-faced Rooster, who gets up each Morning and Crows about his Winning the Election, as if that were an Instant Winning Ticket to Obtaining a RIGHTEOUS Government, which has the POWER to Correct Things that have gone WRong. For Example, Dr. Obama was going to make Changes that we could all Believe in — such as the ObamaScare Healthcare Plan, whose Advocates Wish that all Young Healthy People might Buy Insurance for Covering the Healthcare Costs of Old Dietary Sinners, who have Totally Disregarded the Basic Laws of Good Health, who Vainly Imagine that some "Magic Pills" or "Shot of Puss" might Cure them of whatever Ails them, when in Fact, they would have to Dramatically Change their Living Habits, and begin to Eat Wholesome Natural Foods and Drinks in Moderation, whereby their Bodies might Help them to Fight Off and Eliminate the GALLONS — yes, the TUBS of LARD and MORBID FILTH that they are Packing around with them: beCause of Starving for True Foods, which they are not even Aware of, beginning with Spiritual Foods! Indeed, they are Hungry all of the Time, even after Eating enough for 3 or 4 People, Volume-wise; but, not enough Proper Nourishment for Feeding a single Baby: beCause their Foods are mostly Cooked DEAD Lifeless JUNK, you might say, which not even a Respectable Hog would Eat! Nevertheless, should a Righteous KING be *Ordering* all such People to Eat Proper Foods, and even be Threatening to Behead whomever Disobeys him? Well, please Check the Following Boxes with Statements that you Agree with: so that you might Discover what your own Beliefs might be, by Chance.

> A-[_] I Agree that it would be a Good Idea for some Righteous King to Inform us concerning which Foods are GOOD to Eat, and which ones are BAD, which no Elected President has ever Done: beCause they are Working for the Military Industrial Agribusiness Congressional News Media Bankers' Complex, which is Set Up Perfect for Medical Doctors and Drug Stores. Indeed, the Legal Drug Business is the Biggest Business in America, which Rakes in no less than 2 Trillion Dollars per Year on the Sales of Legal Drugs, plus 2 Trillion or more on Illegal Drugs: beCause Americans are Addicted to Satan's Lies and Deceptions. †§‡

> B-[_] I Believe that it is just a Matter of Time when most People will come to Realize that Medical Doctors are their Worst Enemies — not for Repairing the Abused Victims of Capitalist Car Accidents, nor Setting Broken Bones Straight; but, for Failing to Inform them about the Human Body, and HOW it is Designed to Heal itself, with or without any Drugs, even as all of the Wild Animals have been Healing themselves for millions of Years without the Assistance of any Medical Doctors. †§‡ {See www.Amazon.com for: **"Did God or Satan Ordain Medical Doctors??" (Ask Huck Finn and/or Nigger Jim: because neither Tom Sawyer nor Judge Thatcher would Know!) By The Worldwide People's Revolution!® Book 022.**}

C-[_] I Confess that I am Ignorant about all such Things. However, I do Know for a FACT that the American Bisons roamed on the Great Plains for thousands of Years without the Assistance of any Witchdoctors, nor any Drugs of any Kinds. Therefore, how did they Maintain Good Health without those Drugs?

D-[_] Drugs are GOOD, or else Jesus would have said that they are BAD in *Revelation 18:23—24.* †§‡§§ (NOTE: *Sorceries* meant *Druggeries* at the Time of Christ. In other words, all Nations were Deceived by the Abundance of Babylon's DRUGS. And that is the Reality of it, no matter HOW the Verse is Translated. Only one Translation is Correct in that Case, and it is not Popular. Red Jews are the Chief Drug Manufacturers. It is a HUGE Business, followed by Red Jew Weapons Manufacturers. And those are Facts. Just Follow the Money Trail, and you will Discover that it almost always Leads Back to those Lying Red Jews of *"the Synagogue of Satan,"* just as Jesus stated in *Revelation 2:9 and 3:9,* which can be and must be Proven in a Courtroom. Therefore, those Verses alone make Jesus Christ a True Prophet, and a *Conspiracy Theorist,* according to *Wikipedia.* ‡)

E-[_] Educated People Know for a Fact that Jesus Christ never did Prescribe any Drugs for the People that he Healed. However, he did say, *"They who are Whole need not a Physician; but, they who are Sick."* (See *Matthew 9:12 and Luke 5:31, KJV.*) Therefore, as a Physician with a Good Education with a Capital E, I would say that it is Fair to say that there is a Time and a Place for all Creatures and Characters, including Medical Doctors, who can be either Good or Bad, according to their Beliefs. For Example, Doc Adams of Gunsmoke Fame would not be Charging Poor People 100$ for a 5-minute Conference in his Office; but, he might Accept a Bag of Kale Greens from someone's Garden, in Exchange for his Good Advice; while some Modern Medical Doctors might Charge a thousand Dollars for a 15-minute Operation, or even as much 10,000$, if they Discover that someone does not have any Insurance: beCause they seem to have Dead Consciences. And other Doctors would Charge 10,000$ for the Operation, if they Discovered that a Patient happened to have Insurance, and especially ObamaScare Insurance. †§‡§§

F-[_] The Fact of the Matter is that Healthcare should be FREE, and would be FREE, if a Righteous KING were in Charge of Things: beCause he would Establish Fasting Sanitariums for all Sick and Diseased People, where they could Recover without going into Debt, which Sanitariums would be Supported by the FREEWILL TITHES and Offerings of the People who LOVE such a Good Government, even as Moses Operated his Good Government, and without any Taxes. ‡

G-[_] God Knows that if a Person gets Sick, and Stops Eating, he or she is not Able to Work; and therefore, such a Person would get FIRED from his or her Job, if the Medical Doctor did not Write an Excuse for him or her to Present to the Employer, which no Medical Doctor would do for anyone who might be FASTING: because no Good Doctors Believe in Fasting; but, only in Magic DRUGS! †§‡§§

H-[_] All such Medical Doctors should be Hanged, if they do not Agree that Fasting is the one and only Natural Cure for whatever might Ail most People, who have not been Wounded, who are only Sick or Diseased. †§‡

I-[_] Innocent People know that the Great Physician is Jesus Christ, who is Able and Willing to Heal whomever Believes and Obeys him, which does Require some FAITH; but, not any Drugs: beCause all Drugs are Inventions of Satan and Sons, Incorporated, which can easily be Proven in a Courtroom. †§‡

01-[_] And the SUPREME RULER spoke to Moses and Aaron, saying:

02-[_] When a Man, Woman, or Child shall have in the Skin of his or her Flesh a Rising, a Scab, or a Bright Spot, and it is in the Skin of his or her Flesh like the Plague of Leprosy, or Cancer; then he or she shall be brought to Aaron, the High Priest, or unto one of his Sons who are also Priests, who have this Duty;

03-[_] and the Priest shall Look on the Plague in the Skin of the Flesh, and Study it Carefully; and when the Hair in the Plague has Turned White, and the Plague in his Sight is Deeper than the Surface of the Skin of his or her Flesh, it is a Plague of Leprosy, or a Cancer; and the Priest shall Look on him or her, and Pronounce him or her to be Unclean, and thus he shall Quarantine the Diseased Person for seven Days, without Foods nor Water; but, only with Fresh Fruit Juices, even as the Diseased Person has an Appetite for those Juices, who may Consume as much as he or she Wants to Drink.

04-[_] However, if the Bright Spot is Whitish in the Skin of his or her Flesh, and in Sight is not Deeper than the Skin, and the Hair thereof has not Turned White; then the Priest shall Shut him or her up in a Private Room, who has the Plague, for seven Days, with nothing but Pure Water to Drink in Moderation;

05-[_] and the Priest shall Look on him or her during the Seventh Day; and, behold, if the Plague in his Sight has Stayed in Place, and has not Spread abroad in the Skin, then the Priest shall Shut him or her up for another seven Days without Food nor Water, in order to give the Body an Opportunity to Heal itself: because everyone's Body is always Attempting to Heal itself, and Eliminate any Poisons, Filth, or Accumulations of Waste Matter;

06-[_] and after that Time, the Priest shall Look on him or her again during the Seventh Day; and, behold, if the Plague is somewhat Dark, and the Plague has not Spread in the Skin, the Priest shall Pronounce him Clean: because it is a Scab that shall eventually Fall Off in Time; and thus he or she shall Eat an Abundance of Fresh Sweet Ripe Fruits, and Flush Out his or her Bowels with those Fruits and Fruit Juices; and afterwards he or she shall Wash his or her Body and Clothes with Soap and Water, and thus be Clean.

07-[_] However, if the Scab should Spread itself very much abroad in the Skin, after he or she has been Seen and Treated by the Priest for his or her Cleansing by Fasting and Flushing his or her Bowels Out, he or she shall be Inspected by the Priest, once again: because his or her Body has not yet Thoroughly Cleansed itself;

08-[_] and if the Priest Sees that, and Records the Conditions of the Diseased Person in his Record Book, and Notices that the Scab has Spread itself in the Skin, then the Priest shall Pronounce that Person to be Unclean: because it is a Cancer or Leprosy, which Requires the Patient to have more Patience in the Fasting Sanitarium, and perhaps do a lot of Fasting and Praying, until it goes Away.

09-[_] Indeed, when the Plague of Leprosy or Cancer is in a Man, then he shall be brought to the Priest for his Inspection, no matter where the Cancer might Arise, even in his Private Parts: because it is the Duty of the Priests to Care for the Health of the People, both Physically, Mentally, and Spiritually;

10-[_] and therefore, the Priest shall See him or her in all of his or her Nakedness; and, behold, if the Rising is White in the Skin, and it has Turned the Hairs White, and there is Oozing Raw Flesh in the Rising,

11-[_] it is an Old Leprosy or Cancer in the Skin of his Flesh, and thus the Priest shall Pronounce that Person to be Unclean, who must then be Committed to the Fasting Sanitarium, until he or she is made Clean, even if it Requires a Year or more to be Cleansed: beCause it is an Old Cancer that was within the Body for Years, which just now Appeared on the Skin for a Warning Sign, which must not be Ignored. Indeed, just a simple Pimple on the Skin is also a Warning Sign that the Internal Parts of the Bowels are Poisoned, and must be Cleansed by Fasting.

12-[_] And thus, whomever has a Sore, and especially an Oozing Sore, should Understand that he or she is Unclean, who should Commit him or herself to a Fasting Sanitarium, whereby he or she can be Healed from whatever Ails him or her, and thus be Restored to Good Health, just by Following **"The Proper RULES for FASTING!" (The Complete Instruction Manual for True Repentance!)** Book 046. (See *Leviticus 13* in whatever Version you like.)

J-[_] The Teachings of Jesus Christ have nothing to do with Good Health: beCause Professing "Christians" are the Sickest People on the Earth, while Hindu Fakirs are the Healthiest: because they spend most of the Lives Fasting. †§‡

K-[_] King Jesus would Order all of the People, Worldwide, to Eat Wholesome Natural Foods in Moderation, and would Humiliate anyone who did not Obey him. †§‡

L-[_] Lots of Laughs! King Jesus could not Persuade even ONE Person to Obey him concerning any Subject. However, if you Doubt it, just Study the Life of any Professing "Christian," who normally Eats with the Dogs and Hogs, and Plays with the Skunks and Snakes. †§‡§§

M-[_] Medical Doctors are mostly only Interested in the Bottom Line, which is MONEY: beCause that is WHY they went to Medical Schools — NOT for the Sake of Healing Sick People, even though a Rare Medical Doctor might Profess to Believe in being Charitable. However, he has Insurance Bills to Pay, and many Living Expenses, just like the remainder of us Tax Slaves. Therefore, he must Earn a Fair Amount of Money, just to

(It is Time for some Sane Person to get Control of this Insane World!)

Stay in Business. But, to Charge someone 10,000$ for a 15-minute Operation is Pure ROBBERY, even if that Doctor has Special Skills, which would be like a Politician Charging 100,000$ for a one-hour Speech, who should be made into a Saint! †§‡§§

N-[_] It is Necessary for a Righteous King to Execute True Justice for all of the People, or else he is NOT a True King.

O-[_] Does a King not have any Options? Can he not just Enforce the Laws that are Confined to his Domain, only? For Example, the Elected King of **"The New RIGHTEOUS One-World Government,"** would have to Enforce the Laws in: **"The CONSTITUTION for the New RIGHTEOUS One-World GovernMINT,"** and nothing more, while an Elected King of a Swanky Castle would have to Obey and Enforce the Laws and Rules of the Constitution for that Swanky Fortress, only. Therefore, if someone does not Like the Laws nor the Rules of his or her Fortress, he or she will be Provided with Free Transportation to Move to one that he or she does Like, if he or she cannot Persuade the People within that Fortress to Change their Laws: so that he or she might be Happy. ‡

P-[_] People like to Complain, just to get Attention, if nothing else. However, if People had their own **"Beautiful Swanky PALACES"** to Live in, they would have very little to Complain about: beCause each Father would be the King of his own Castle, you might say, who could do his Gardening as he might Please, and thus make a Paradise for himself and his Family, according to his Skills and Abilities. Otherwise, he could Invite **"The Swanky Association of Professional Gardeners"** to take Good Care of his Garden, in Exchange for a certain Amount of Produce. ‡

Q-[_] And what about the Queens of their Castles? Perhaps the Queens should be giving the Orders in those Swanky Palaces?

R-[_] Well, the King of the Castle could give his Queen Permission to make any Decisions around the House, or even concerning the Gardening, if she is Good at it; but, the Home-craft Workshop and Sales Shop should be his Responsibility, and his Wife and Children should Obey him, whereby there can be Peace in that Family. Indeed, if such a Husband Checks the above Box, and his Potential Wife does not Like that Plan, she should not Marry him. But, if she has already Married him, she should Love and Obey him, just as the *Scriptures* Demand: beCause it is the LAW of GOD. ‡

S-[_] I am not going to make a Slave of myself, just to Please some Silly King.

T-[_] Just Think — if everyone in the Whole World should Learn, Believe, Love, and OBEY the Master Plan of our Elected King, we would all be Moderately RICH within 20 Years or less! Therefore, it is Wise of us to Teach that Great Truth to all of the Children, whereby they might be Inspired to Learn, Believe, Love, and OBEY his Master Plan! †§‡

U-[_] I Understand what you are Saying. However, getting the Masses of People to Agree is another Major Problem, which is not going to be Solved by any Dimwitcrats nor Reprobates in Washington, even though they could all Agree to Print and Publish this

Inspired Book, and place a Copy of it in every American Mailbox, Worldwide, with this Return Address:

**The Worldwide People's Revolution!®
C/O The President of the United States
1600 Pennsylvania Avenue
Washington, D.C., U.S.A. 20500**

V-[_] That would Cost too much. Taxpayers would Object to the Costs. Queen Victoria would be Greatly Upset. Wall Street Bankers would be Pooping in their Pants. Businesses would be Boarded Up, and the People would be Shocked. The Stock Market would CRASH! And we Work Slaves would be the Victims of Capitalism, again!

W-[_] World War 3 would Break Out!

X-[_] X-amount of People would Love it, and thus Promote it, which would Cause a Real Bloodless REVOLUTION, which would be GOOD!

Y-[_] You might Love it; but, I would HATE it: beCause I have spent 40 Years Fighting Communism and Socialism, and your Elected King is Promoting the Purest Form of Communism and Socialism, whereby he Promotes a Dictatorship! HEIL HITLER! †§‡§§

Z-[_] Even a Zebra can Understand that someone must be in Charge of Things, or else we get what we Presently have, which is Worse than Communism, Socialism, and Fascism: beCause we American Tax Slaves are now more than 147 Trillion Dollars in DEBT! Yes, Ask Bill Moyers, if you Doubt it. Educate yourselves, O Ostriches, and Stop Hiding your Heads in the Sand. †§‡

09-02 [_] President Obama had to Bail Out the Bankers, or else they would have Crashed our Great False Economy, and we would all now be Standing Impatiently in Long Soup Lines, except for those Rich Red Jew Bankers, who would be Laughing at us Ignorant Fools. †§‡

09-03 [_] Our Elected King would have allowed all of those Red Jew Bankers to go OUT of Business, and would have Pushed them Over the Cliff, himself: beCause Bankers are not Needed for True Prosperity. Yes, ask King Solomon, if you Doubt it. ‡

09-04 [_] Powerless Presidents are Political PUPPETS on the Strings of Red Jew Bankers. Indeed, who is it that does not Know that the "Federal Reserve Bank" has been Owned and Operated by Lying Red Jews before and after its Conception on Jekyll Island, in 1913? Indeed, it is a Privately-owned Red Jew Bank, which is neither a Reserve, nor a Federal Government Bank: beCause the Federal Government does not have a Bank. Read your Constitution. (See YouTube Videos for: "The Creature from Jekyll Island" for more Information. See also *Eustace Mullins, Benjamin Freedman, David Irving, Ernst Zundel* and Related Websites and YouTube Videos, which Expose the Strange Creature from Jekyll Island.) ‡

09-05 [_] Is your Elected King a Conspiracy Theorist? Does he Believe that House Fires Caused World Trade Center Tower 7 to come Crashing Down in less than 7 Seconds, after Heating Up

283 Hardened Steel Columns, some of which were 22-inches by 52-iches by 47 stories tall, which all Collapsed in UNISON, like Ballet Dancers hitting the Floor at the very same Time, as if those House Fires had been Equally Distributed throughout that Great Tower, which covered nearly a whole City Block? Indeed, just ONE of those Steel Columns would have surely Resisted the Collapse, and thus Delayed it; but, behold, not one Steel Column Protested Against it, even as none of the Eyewitnesses during November 22nd, 1963, Protested Against the Warren Commission Report, after making a Full Federal Government Investigation of the President Kennedy Assassination by a Magic Silver Bullet, which was Shot from behind the Picket Fence on the Grassy Knoll in DAL-ass, TEX-ass, which Bullet came from the Dallas Book Depository, which Leapfrogged itself right over the Heads of the Federal Burden of Phony Investigations, as well as the Central Unintelligent Agencies — none of whom Discovered those Eyewitnesses, whereby they might have made Public Testimonies concerning whatever they Saw and Heard during that Fateful Day: beCause the Warren Commission was not Searching for the Whole Truth, and nothing but the Whole Truth: beCause they were Working for the Synagogue of Satan, whom they are still Covering Up: beCause the Whole Truth might Threaten our National Insecurities, and Cause Americans to Realize that their Government is WICKED and EVIL beyond Measure — Thanks to the News Media, which is Controlled by those Lying Red Jews! Otherwise, those News Reporters would DEMAND: **"The Great Worldwide TELEVISED Court HEARING,"** whereby we Tax Slaves might Learn the WHOLE Truth about all Kinds of Important Subjects — that is, IF they have nothing to HIDE! However, they have MUCH to Hide: beCause the Synagogue of Satan is in Control of it, which can easily be Proven in a Courtroom, which has already been Proven in the Public Courtroom of Honest Opinions! Indeed, it has been Reported that 60% or more of Americans do not Believe the Warren Commission Report, nor the 9/11 Commission Report: beCause it was a Classic Case of the Wily Federal Foxes Investigating the Chicken House Incidents. †§‡§§

09-06 [ ] If the President had any Power at all, he could Order those Top Secret Files on the Kennedy Assassination to be Opened and Published, Worldwide, on the Internet: so that everyone might Learn and Know for a Fact that Lee Harvey Oswald was the Sole Assassinator of President Kennedy, who Acted alone with the Assistance of the CIA, who used him for a PATSY, just like he Testified on his Proverbial Deathbed, in DALL-ass, TEX-ass, whose Police DEPARTment Failed to do their Duty to make a FULL and Unbiased Investigation of the Assassination, who also did not Discover more than a hundred Eye-and-Ear Witnesses, who Testified to other more-Honest Investigators that they Heard Shots coming from the Grassy Knoll, which were Echoes coming Off of the Picket Fence, after Leapfrogging over the Heads of the Warren Commission — all of whom have Died Off and gone Straat to HELL! †§‡§§

09-07 [ ] If a Righteous King were in Command, he would Order all such Secret Files to be Opened Up, since the Federal Government of **"The Divided States of United Lies"** Claims to be Innocent of any Wrongdoings in all such Cases as the Kennedy Assassination and the Evil Events of September 11th, 2001. Therefore, if they are Innocent, why are they Afraid of whatever might be Found in those "Top Secret" Documents? After all, there are no less than a Million Unsolved Murders in this Country, and almost anyone with Legal Credentials can get Access to their Files, in order to Study them; but, NOT in the Kennedy Assassination, nor in the Abraham Lincoln Assassination Cover-up Scandal: beCause those Events Involve Lying Red JEWS! †§‡

09-08 [_] An Elected King of **"The New RIGHTEOUS One-World Government"** would have NO Power over anything that Happens in **"The Divided States of United Lies"**: beCause it is Out of his Jurisdiction. Period.

    A-[_] I Agree — no Elected King of a Righteous One-World Government would have any Authority over the Private Affairs of any Particular Nation, including **"The Divided States of United Lies,"** which should be BOMBED OFF of the Earth with Nuclear Weapons for all of their Government Sins against other Nations, and I am NOT a Muslim nor a Hindu. †§‡§§

    B-[_] I Believe in Justice for ALL, including the People of other Nations, who have Heard enough Lies from the United States of America, whose Ignorant People Vainly Imagine that their WICKED Federal Government is Exempt from any Justice. For Example, American Bombers dropped more Bombs on Laos and Cambodia during the Vietnam War, than were dropped during all of World War 2! Moreover, they did it without Declaring War on either of those Nations, including Vietnam, which was some Kind of a "Police Action," which was supposed to Prevent the Communist Domino Effect that Overran China and Russia — Thanks to that Wicked WICKED Karl Marx, who was another Lying Red JEW, who Forgot to Inform his Followers about the Monetary System of a RIGHTEOUS One-World GovernMINT, which has no Use for Red Jew Bankers, much less for Political Puppet Masters in some Shadow Government, which Works Behind the Scenes, whereby no one can Identify WHO is in Charge of anything — such as those Undeclared Wars in Korea, Vietnam, Laos, and Cambodia, which were Unconstitutional. Therefore, I say that if we Elect a Righteous KING to Govern **"The New RIGHTEOUS One-World Government,"** he should have TOTAL Control over EVERYONE, including the Escapees: George Warmonger Bush, Little Dick Chicanery, Condoosleezee Rice Patty, Donald Rummyfell, Paul Wolfwits, Allan Greenspandex, and all of the other Associates of those Red Jew Conspirators in the District of Criminals! †§‡

    C-[_] I Confess that some Responsible Intelligent Person should be in Control of **"The New RIGHTEOUS One-World Government!"** However, to have TOTAL Control of everyone in the World is another Subject, which Frightens me: beCause People have been known to Change their Minds, and even become Cruel Tax Masters, Crusaders, and Chief Criminals, themselves — such as that Wicked Adolf Hitler, who put millions of those Lying Red Jews into Concentration Camps, and then Personally Tortured them without Condoms on his Tally Whacker, whereby some of them Bled to Death through their Mouths, after being Sodomized in their Ears, whereby they are still giving Contradictory False Testimonies in Courtrooms, if you can Believe it! Yes, they are still Lying about it, saying that the Nazis put 4 or 5 Bodies in just ONE Crematory Oven every 10 Minutes, when even an Ignorant Idiot would Know that Hard Enamel TEETH cannot be made into Ashes in less than 4 Hours, which anyone can Prove by Cremating a Hog's Head in their own Oven at Home, at 4000 °F, which is more than 13 Times as much Heat as it Requires for Baking Cookies. And I am a Lying Red Jew, who should be brought to Court! †§‡§§

    D-[_] Damn it, why does the Chief Editor allow such Sarcastic Nonsense to get Published in a Good Book like this, which could Ruin it? DUMBmocracy should Vote against it, and Outlaw it: because it is NOT Democratic, much less Decent Literature for Children

(It is Time for some Sane Person to get Control of this Insane World!)

and Spiritual Dwarfs to Study, who might even DEMAND: **"The Great Worldwide TELEVISED Court HEARING,"** just to Learn the Whole Truth about the HoloHOAX! Yes, I would like to Know whether or not an Adult Human Body could be Cremated every 10 Minutes in any Oven; and, if so, we would only have to have 5 such Ovens to Cremate all of the Remaining Lying Red Jews in the World within ONE DAY: beCause, for some Strange Reason, none of them Checked any of these Boxes: beCause they Obviously do NOT Agree with such Statements, which would have to be Broken Down into PARTS that they do Agree with. For Example:

01-[_] I Agree that a Nazi Crematory Oven was a Standard Traditional Size, having enough Space for ONE Adult Body, less than 20-inches in Diameter, or else such a Body would not Fit through the Doorway of the Retort. ‡

02-[_] I Agree that it might have been Possible to Cremate 2 Small Bodies at the same Time in one Nazi Retort; but, not 3, 4, nor 5 of them. ‡

03-[_] I Agree that Lying Red Jews have a Tendency to Exaggerate Things in their Favor, which has been Proven by Court Records around the World. ‡

04-[_] I Agree that X-amount of Jews, Gypsies, Homosexuals, and other Victims of the Nazi Jews, who were in Charge of the Concentration Camps, did in Fact DIE from Various Sicknesses, Diseases, Murders by Fellow Prisoners, and Exposure to Bad Weather Conditions. ‡

05-[_] I Agree that it would Require one Hour just to Cool Off a Crematory Oven before the Door could Safely be Opened: beCause of the Intense Heat within it.

06-[_] I Agree that it would Require at least an Hour to Heat Up the Oven before a Body could be put into it, if it were a Cold Oven.

07-[_] I Agree that it was a Sanitary Method of Disposing of Dead Bodies, and especially Diseased Bodies, whereby such Diseases could not Spread so easily.

08-[_] I Agree that People could have been Dying on the Trains, before they Arrived at the Prison Camps, whereby Crematoriums would be Required for Disposing of those Bodies.

09-[_] I Agree that there were only 2 Great Smoking Chimneys at Auschwitz, Poland, in the Nazi Concentration Camp, which was a Work Camp.

10-[_] I Agree that a Chimney must have Sufficient Space for Exhausting the Fumes that come from a Retort.

11-[_] I Agree that if a Chimney did not have Sufficient Space for Exhausting the Fumes, the Fire would be Choked Out to some Degree, and thus the Oven would not get Sufficiently Hot enough to Cremate a Human Body.
12-[_] I Agree that I do not know much about Crematories.

85

A-[_] I am a Professional Expert concerning this Subject.
B-[_] I am not an Expert; but, I do know something about Crematories.
C-[_] I am a Holocaust Survivor.
D-[_] I am a Dunce when it comes to Knowing the Actual Facts.
E-[_] I am an Educated Person concerning this Subject, who has "red" many Books about it.
F-[_] I am not Interested in the Facts.
G-[_] God knows that I Want to Learn the Whole Truth about the Holocaust, even if I am Proven to be WRong.
H-[_] Hell will freeze over before I Confess what I Know about the Holocaust.
I-[_] Nazi Crematories were just Standard Crematories of the Time.
J-[_] Nazi Crematories were especially Designed for handling huge numbers of Bodies, daily, which can be Proven in a Courtroom.
K-[_] All of the Evidences were Destroyed by the Nazis concerning the Holocaust.
L-[_] Lots of Laughs! NONE of the Evidence was Destroyed about the HoloHOAX. All of the Records were Preserved, and they Contradict the Red Jew LIES about it, which is WHY those Records were kept Secret for 50+ Years, just like the Documents for the Kennedy Assassination Cover-up: because the same People are in Charge of it!
M-[_] Money was the Motive.
N-[_] No Photos of the Insides of the Crematories have been Preserved.
O-[_] You are Lying: because many Photos have been Preserved.
P-[_] Those Lying Red Jews do not Want us to See the Photos of Nazi Prison Camps, much less the thousands of Record Books.
Q-[_] The German Company that Designed the Crematoriums have Detailed Drawings and Blueprints with Explanations.
R-[_] Records Reveal that Red Jews are LIARS, which is WHY they are Called "Red" Jews, instead of Honest White Jews, like Jesus Christ and our Elected King.
S-[_] Saints were never in the Business of making Wars. Saints do not Resist Evils: beCause they Trust in God to Judge and Reward them Correctly.
T-[_] The Total Number of Victims of the Holocaust, according to the Red Cross, which also Kept Meticulous Records, was less than 190,000. ‡
U-[_] The Ovens did not Cremate any Adult Bodies within 10 Minutes, nor even one Hour: beCause that is Impossible. ‡
V-[_] The True Victims of the Holocaust are those Ignorant People who Believe all such Red Jew LIES as one can find in the Holocaust Museum in the District of Criminals, in Washington.
W-[_] World War 2 was Provoked by the British and French, who Refused to Debate the Issues of the Time with Adolf Hitler.
X-[_] X-amount of People Sincerely Believe that 6 to 16 Million Jews Died in the Holocaust, in spite of the Fact that there were less than 20 Million Jews in the whole World at that Time, according to the World

(It is Time for some Sane Person to get Control of this Insane World!)

Almanac, who somehow Multiplied in Astronomical Numbers just after the War, disregarding the Fact that most Jews were too Old, too Young, or not even Married! Indeed, even Today, the Jews have a Growth Rate of about 1.3%, or just barely enough to keep them from becoming Extinct! Indeed, the Jews have one of the Lowest Birth Rates of any Race of People on the Earth. Therefore, what are the Chances of them Multiply at a Birth Rate of 49.7 percent from 1945—1949, when the Census was taken? †§‡

Y-[_] Whatever the Facts are, it would be Interesting to Learn them: so that Young People are not Misled by False Information.

Z-[_] The Zeal of **The Worldwide People's Revolution!**® will make those Facts Known to all Nations.

E-[_] The Elected King of **"The New RIGHTEOUS One-World Government"** should have Total Authority to Expose the Sins of any Nation that does not Cheerfully Agree to get RID of all Weapons of Mass Destruction: beCause they are Demon-possessed People.

F-[_] I Fail to Understand WHY all Nations would not Cheerfully get Rid of their Aggressive Weapons, just to Prove that they are not Warmongers?

G-[_] God Knows that if Nigger Jim has a Club, Tom Sawyer must have a Pistol; and if Tom has a Pistol, it should be Stolen by Huck Finn's Pappy: beCause he might Need it for Robbing the Bank, since the Bank is not Interested in Helping him nor Huck Finn to Earn an Honest Living, whereby they might not be made into Criminals, just to Survive. ‡

H-[_] Honest People and Righteous Governments would not Object to Attending **"The Great Worldwide TELEVISED Court HEARING"**: beCause they have nothing to Hide, nor anything to Lose by Helping to Establish **"The New RIGHTEOUS One-World Government,"** which would only make Life much Better for all of the People, Worldwide. After all, we do not Lack any Mountains of Rocks for Doing that; but, we are Quickly Running OUT of Cheap Energy for getting the Work Done. ‡

I-[_] I say that if our Elected King is the most Righteous Man that we can Discover, he is Qualified to make the Final Decisions about any Subjects: beCause of his Wisdom, which is a Gift from God.

J-[_] Justice Demands that all Nations should be Assisted to become Moderately Rich, if they Choose to Do so; and all Good People will Choose to Do so: beCause it is the Best Way to Solve our Massive Problems, including those Hateful Terrorist Attacks, which a Righteous King can easily Control. {See: **"Terrorists Beware that your Days are Numbered!" (HOW to Bring those Terrorist Attacks to a Screeching HALT!) By The Worldwide People's Revolution!**® Book 043.}

K-[_] No King can Control those Radical Islamic Muslim Murderers, even if he is a Riichus King: beCause none of those People will Agree to Attend **"The Great**

Worldwide TELEVISED Court HEARING": beCause they Know for a Fact that they could never Stand Up to **"The Swanky Sword of Divine Truths!" (The Most Powerful Weapon in the Whole Universe!) By The Worldwide People's Revolution!®** Book 067. Indeed, they would be Defeated within a Minute or 2, if they could not Prove that they have not been Murdering Innocent People. †§‡

L-[_] Lots of Laughs! ISIS is the Israeli Secret Instigation Services, who can do no WRong. Indeed, they have the Approval of the Saudi Arabians, who Support them with Money and Weapons, which **"The Divided States of United Lies"** SELLS to the Arabians: beCause they are our FRIENDS! Yes, those Weapons are Manufactured by the Israelis, and Bought by the United States, and Resold to the Saudis, whereby everyone stands to Gain some Wealth — except the Victims of ISIS Aggressions, which are not as many as the Victims of the Dictator of Syria, whose Name is Bashar al Assad, who is a Muslim Saint, who Bombs his own People, who is Supported by the Russians and Iranians, who Pretend to be the Enemies of ISIS, who is Defending the Poor People of Syria, who are getting Bombed by Assad and the Iranians and Russians, who are our Enemies: beCause they do Mean Things to Innocent People. Therefore, it has become a very Complicated MESS in the Middle East. †§‡§§

M-[_] It would not be a Mess for very long, if we Tax Slaves DEMANDED **"The Great Worldwide TELEVISED Court HEARING,"** whereby we might Learn all Sides of all such Issues, and thus draw up some Rational Conclusions — such as Helping each Group of Antagonists to Build their own **"GLORIOUS Swanky Hotels Castles and Fortresses,"** after they have Filled Out and Filed **"The Complete SURVEYS of our VALUES,"** whereby we might Decide WHERE they all Belong, if not in HELL! †§‡§§

N-[_] Not everyone will Want to become Moderately RICH: beCause of Believing that it will Ruin them. After all, it is easier for a Camel to squeeze through the Eye of a Needle, than for a Rich Man to Enter into the Holy Kingdom of All that is GOOD with his Trainload of Nuclear Weapons. †§‡

O-[_] I am getting Sick and Tired of this Nonsense. Therefore, let me Opt Out.

09-09 [_] A Powerless President cannot become a Tyrant, like some Elected King, who might have a Worm Turn Over in his Brains, and thus take a Notion to Drop Hydrogen Bombs on all Major Cities, Worldwide, just to Reduce the Population, even though there is Plenty of Space in this World of Wonders for at least a hundred Times as many People, who would have to STOP Building those Ugly Highways, Parking Lots, Shopping Mauls, Ball Parks, and all such Needless Things. Indeed, they would have to take up Gardening, according to: **"The LUSCIOUS All-Mineral Organic Method of Gardening!" (HOW to Grow DELICIOUS Satisfying Foods for Potential Kingz and Kweenz in Swanky PALACES!) By The Worldwide People's Revolution!®** Book 021. †§‡§§

09-10 [_] A Righteous King would never Do any such Evil Things, nor would he make it Possible for anyone else to Do any such Evil Things, if he were Given the Power to Manage his

(It is Time for some Sane Person to get Control of this Insane World!)

Government the Way that he Wants to, which would be Free of all such Hateful Weapons: beCause they are not Needed for True Prosperity. ‡

— Chapter 10 —

Fair Warnings!

10-01 [_] Many Scientists and other Professional People have been Warning us for Decades about the DANGERS of Capitalism and the Exploitations of our Natural Resources, which are very Limited, except for Oceans of Water and Mountains of Rocks, Sunlight and Wind, which can be Used Wisely for making almost everyone Moderately RICH, without Telling any Lies nor Selling any Trash. Therefore, why Continue to make Fools of ourselves, and all for the Sake of PRIDE, just to ride around in those Stinking Noisy Polluting CARS, Pickups, Vans, Trucks, Buses, Motorboats, Motorcycles, Motor Scooters, Lawnmowers, Snowmobiles, 4-Wheelers, and whatever else, which are like Children's Toys, which Spiritual Adults should Grow Out of. After all, we have Tested the Madness of Capitalism, Communism, Socialism, Fascism, and other Isms, and have Discovered that they are all Economic Disasters, which have Lowered our Standards of Living by many Degrees from the 1600's, whereby few People have Good Health, and most People Suffer with Diseases, Drug Addictions, Poverty, Crimes, Wars, Tax Burdens, Prisons, and whatever. Indeed, it is Truly a Sad Disgusting Long List of Stories for the History Books, which makes the Ancient Civilizations seem to be less Barbaric than this Generation of Evildoers, even though it also Appears that we have made some Progress in Reducing the Burdens of the Work Slaves: beCause of the Inventions of Tractors, Trucks, and all such Helpful Tools, without Realizing how Wonderful Life could have been for everyone with less Expenses, Pollutions, Crimes, and Corruptions in Governments, just by Building those **"GLORIOUS Swanky Hotels Castles and Fortresses!" (Beautiful Planned City States for WISE Intelligent Well-Educated People with Common Sense and Good Understanding!) By The Worldwide People's Revolution!®** Book 019.

10-02 [_] O Elected King, it is a Great Shame that our Founding Fathers did not Think about the Great Opportunities that were at Hand when they were writing up their Constitution: because they would have no doubt Decided to Establish **"The New RIGHTEOUS One-World Government!" (HOW to Establish a Righteous One-World Government without Going to WAR!)** Yes, most of the Nations would have probably Cooperated with them at that Time, if they had just began to Build those **"Beautiful Swanky PALACES!" (A New Concept in Living Habits — Swanky Palaces for Poor People!)** After all, just ONE such Palace would Persuade any Sane Person that it is the Right Way to go.

10-03 [_] O Elected King, if we, the People, Fail to Heed the many Voices of Scientists, who are Warning us about Climate Changes and Melting Icebergs, we are likely to Pay the Ultimate Price with our own Lives: beCause it is Possible for the Magnetic Poles to SHIFT, whereby **"The Divided States of United Lies"** might end up in the same Position as Siberia, or the Sahara

Desert in Africa, or God knows WHERE! Indeed, it could even Inspire the Mountains to become Valleys, and the Valleys of the Oceans to become Mountains, whereby most of Mankind would be TRASHED! ‡

10-04 [_] Well, we never know what a single Day might bring forth; but, we are like Children who are Playing with Fire, who do not Realize what a Great Fire can be Kindled by a single Spark! And thus Capitalism has Dug its own Grave, you might say, if those Scientists are Correct about the Results of Trillions of Tons of Wastes in our Atmosphere, which is Totally Unnatural, even though some People Argue that Beneficial Volcanoes put more Pollution into the Atmosphere. § However, it is a Different Kind of Pollution, which is not nearly so Harmful as Solvents, Paint Thinners, Pesticides, Herbicides, and a whole List of Chemical Abominations, much of which comes from the Production of CARS, which are Chief Offenders — Thanks to that Lazy Son of Satan in **"The BIG White OUTHOUSE on the Not-so-Biblical Capitol DUNGHILL!" (The Chief Sins of the Divided States of United Lies!)** Book 023. ‡

10-05 [_] So, O Elected King, when we Reluctantly Add Up all of the Massive Problems with the Environment, the Great False Economy, the Wasted Gas, the Insane Wars, the Weapons of Mass Destruction, the Sicknesses, Diseases, Drugs, Doctor Bills, Insurance Scams, Taxes, and all of the EVILS of Capitalism, it is very Depressing, and almost Hopeless, which is no doubt WHY many People have Committed Suicide, while many more have Tried and Failed, which is NOT a Good Record for the Books of Remembrance. Indeed, there are Court Records by Trainloads, which Prove that we Human Beings have GOOFED UP. Therefore, it is now Time for a Drastic and Dramatic Change in our Thinking and Acting, before the next Big Crisis does us Under! After all, none of us are Prepared for Survival, if the Sunlight Refuses to Shine for several Years: beCause of something that Happens in the Sky, which is Beyond our Control. †§‡

10-06 [_] Well, I have been Preaching about the Goodness and Great Advantages of those **"GLORIOUS Swanky Hotels Castles and Fortresses"** for more than 30 Years, without any Great Success: beCause of several Reasons.

> A-[_] I have not had the millions nor billions of dollars that Politicians and Drug Companies have had, whereby I might do some Advertising.
>
> B-[_] What I am Proposing is a Great Threat to the Evil Empire, and especially to the Polluters and Producers of Abominations.
>
> C-[_] My Master Plan calls for HARD WORK, when Compared with Playing Money Games, or Running a Computer, even though the Hardest Work will still be Easier and much more Enjoyable than many Occupations — such as Cleaning Out the Sewage Systems, Gathering Chickens in a Huge Chicken House, and Working at 90 MpH in some Factory that can never Produce enough to make the Boss Happy.
>
> D-[_] My Literature has a lot of Capitalized Words in it, which Turns Off a lot of "educated" People, who would not Capitalize Bite, even if Alligators took Big Bites out of their Rumps.
>
> E-[_] My Literature seems to Bother the Consciences of Guilty People, who are Offended by the Truth concerning any given Subject.

(It is Time for some Sane Person to get Control of this Insane World!)

F-[_] Religious People, who have Studied the *Scriptures* just enough to Puff Up their Minds with Great Pride, are Sure that my New MAGNIFIED Version is Inspired by Satan, and not by the Hebrew God: beCause my Version is not an Exact Quote of their Favorite Version, which they Site as PROOF that I am the Anti-Christ, The BEAST, the False Prophet, or all 3 in one Unholy Trinity!

G-[_] Some People say that if God was on my Side, that he would Bless me with an Abundance of Riches, whereby I could Build my own Swanky Fortress, even if I had to Hire some Poor Mexican Slaves to get it Done.

H-[_] Some People say that they need to SEE my Face, just to Decide whether or not my Words are True or False, even though they will Confess that they have not Seen the Face of Jesus, Peter, James, John, nor Paul — all of whom they Trust, even if their Words are Contradictory.

I-[_] Some People say that it is just not the Right TIME for the Construction of Swanky Fortresses, which might have Worked Well before the Invention of Gunpowder and Bombs; but, those same People just Ignore the 4,999 other Good Reasons for Building such Fortresses, which would Certainly be much Safer to Live in than their Poisonous Wooden / Plastic Firetrap Mouse-infested Cockroach Dens, which are about as Secure as Paper Tents in a Tornado.

J-[_] Some People say that if I do not Dress like them, I am not one of them; and therefore, I cannot be Accepted among them, even though they will also Confess that Jesus Christ does not Dress like them, nor did most People for at least 5,000 Years.

K-[_] Some People say that I should Condense my Master Plan to no more than 5 Books of no more than 200 Pages, each: because hardly anyone will be Willing to Read 350+ Books, which would be like reading 20 Bibles from Cover to Cover, which only one Person in 100,000 has ever Managed to do; but, I tell them that the Reason for that is the Boringness of all such Books, or perhaps the Foolishness within them, while my Inspired Books have Genuine Solutions that no one can Prove to be WRong, nor Unworkable. †§‡

L-[_] Some People say that my Books have far too much Humor in them, which Causes People to Laugh at them, rather than Laugh with them; but, I tell them that more People Complain about a LACK of Humor in them. Therefore, there is no Way to Please everyone. †§‡

M-[_] Some People say that my Books Cost too much Money, and should be Free on the Internet; but, I tell them that I already Tried that Plan, and only one Person Contributed anything to my Cause during 20 Years! Therefore, that Plan is not Workable for someone who does not even get a Social Security Check.

N-[_] Some People say that my Books deal with Non-Issues of the Time — such as Religious Nonsense; but, I tell them that what is Nonsense to one Person, is the Heart and

Soul of Enlightenment to another Person, who can hardly wait to Discover what is in the next Chapter.

O-[_] Some People say that my Opinions do not Mean anything to them: because I do not have a College Degree; but, then I Remind them that Jesus never even went to School, and he is Hailed as the KING of Kings!

P-[_] Some People say that my Principles are Low Class, Old Fashioned, and Irrelevant to our Time; but, I tell them that Jesus Christ is the SAME, both Yesterday, Today and Forever, which sometimes Causes them to Spit of him, Verbally, as if they were Superior in some Way, while he might be Inferior, even though they have yet to Walk on the Water behind him.

Q-[_] Some People say that they Question my Motives: beCause they are not Quite Sure that I am Seeking their Good Health, Peace of Mind, nor True Prosperity, in spite of the Fact that my entire Master Plan can be carried out without my Presence. Indeed, I could Die, and the Plan would still be Workable, if People just Acted Wisely and Followed my Instructions, and Elected a Righteous King to Govern them.

R-[_] Some People say that they do not Believe in Reincarnation, even though they will Confess in a Courtroom that it would have been Impossible for Jesus Christ to be Resurrected without the Act of Reincarnation, which is a Spirit Re-entering into a Body.

S-[_] Some People say that if I were a Saint, they would Believe my Words of Truths; but, I tell them that many Words of Saints have been Rejected by Ignorant Sinners.

T-[_] Some People say that my Testimony about the Visitation of Christ to me in Person is Terribly Flawed: because there were no Eyewitnesses, other than myself; but, I tell them that Elijah had the same Problem.

U-[_] Some People say that I Fail to Understand People: beCause of Living like a Hermit for most of my Life; but, I also tell them, once again, that Elijah had the same Problem.

V-[_] Some People say that I am a Victim of Self Pity, and should Stop Feeling Sorry for myself, even though I Greatly Feel Sorry for them: beCause they are among the Deprived People, who have never Experienced the JOYS nor Exhilarations that I have Experienced from Writing my Inspired Books, which make me the Happiest Person that I know of!

W-[_] Some People say that the Vietnam War messed up my Mind; but, I Remind them that it was more Beneficial than Detrimental: beCause of all of the Good Lessons that I Learned — one of which is the Fact that the Federal Government of **"The Divided States of United Lies"** cannot be Trusted, who make War against Innocent People, and Fail to make Reparations for all such Chief Sins: beCause they are Lying Hypocrites!

X-[_] X-amount of People say that I am too Negative, and should be more Positive-minded; but, I Remind them that after putting up with their Unbelief for more than 50 Years, I have still not let go of the *Rope of Hope!*

(It is Time for some Sane Person to get Control of this Insane World!)

Y-[_] Some People say that I am a Weeping Vile of Yesteryears, who should Forget about the Injustices of **"The Divided States of United Lies!" (The so-called "United States of North America" in Disguise!)** But, I tell them that without Truths, there is no True Justice; and, without True Justice, there is no Peace; and, without True Peace, those Hateful Wars will never Cease.

Z-[_] Some People say that my Zeal will Destroy me, and perhaps also Destroy them and the Whole World; but, I tell them that without my Zeal for Righteousness, and your Zeal for Justice, also, the World is Guaranteed to be Destroyed by Lawlessness, Corruption in Governments, Selfishness, and GREED!

10-07 [_] O Elected King, I do Hope to God that this is your Last Chapter in this Book, even though it does not have a Conclusion Chapter: beCause a hundred Pages this Size is Sufficient Spiritual Food for one Day, even if it is not the Worst Spiritual Food that I have ever Eaten, you might say; but, it is Good for Passing Time, since my Mind is not Able to Remember much of anything, even if I have Heard it a hundred Times. Indeed, such Books are Rich with Thoughts, which are Worth the Time to Meditate on; but, I seldom Stop to Meditate: because I want to get Finished with the Book, and get on with another one.

10-08 [_] Well, that might Prove to be a Mistake on your Part: beCause, if there is something Good to Meditate on, it is Best to do it at the Time that it crosses your Mind, while it is Fresh in your Mind, whereby you will get much more out of it, which will Help to Satisfy your Soul.

10-09 [_] O Elected King, I can Think of a thousand Questions that you have not yet Answered within this Book, which might Require another hundred Pages, or more, and still not Satisfy my Soul: beCause I am Starved for Truths. Nevertheless, I Trust that your other Inspired Books will be Answering those Questions about a RIGHTEOUS One-World Government. For Example, will **"The New RIGHTEOUS One-World Government"** Intervene in the Affairs of Swanky Fortresses, and Speak Evil of Potential Wicked Kings, who may be Elected to Govern them? Will that Government have FBI and Central Intelligence Agencies all around the World?

10-10 [_] NO! The People of each Swanky Fortress will be Responsible for Discovering their own Righteous Kings and Queens. However, if they Ask for Assistance from **"The New RIGHTEOUS One-World Government,"** we may Help them. After all, that Good Government must be a Perfect Example for all other Governments to Follow, which is a very Tall Order, you might say; but, if I am in Charge of it, it will be the Perfect Example: beCause we will Concentrate on it, and Meditate on it, and do our Best to make it a RIICHUS Guvernment.

— Chapter 16 —

A "Long Boring List" of other Fascinating Books by the same Inspired Author!

16-001 [_] **"LIGHTNING Versus the Lightning Bug!"** (HOW almost Everyone can become Moderately RICH, without Telling Any Lies nor Selling Any Trash!) By The Worldwide People's Revolution!® Book 001. The Cover Photo shows a Beautiful Sunrise in the Blest Land of Eternal Springtime!

16-002 [_] **"What is WRong with those Professing Christians?"** (A Self-Examination of the Heart of the Body of Good Government!) By The Worldwide People's Revolution!® Book 002. The Cover Photo shows a Small Portion of our Unfinished Retirement Home.

16-003 [_] **"For the Love of Money!"** (The Strange Things that People Say and Do to Get more Money!) By The Worldwide People's Revolution!® Book 003. The Cover Photo shows a Jewish Boy studying the *Scriptures*.

16-004 [_] **"HOW to Prepare for CLIMATE CHANGES!"** (The Wisest Plan for Mankind to Follow!) By The Worldwide People's Revolution!® Book 004. The Cover Photo shows Dark Awesome Clouds.

16-005 [_] **"WHY do I have to be Surrounded by CRAZY PEOPLE?"** (Do almost all People Feel like they are Surrounded by CRAZY PEOPLE??) By The Worldwide People's Revolution!® Book 005. The Cover Photo shows Delicious Fragrant Ripe Mangos.

16-006 [_] **"The Washington Journal is a FARCE!"** (C-SPAN Managers are not very WISE!) By The Worldwide People's Revolution!® Book 006. The Cover Photo shows a Portion of "Mars," up close.

16-007 [_] **"The PRAYERS of PUMPKINHEADS!"** (Even God Needs a Little Humor to Cheer himself Up!) By The Worldwide People's Revolution!® Book 007. The Cover Photo shows the Author's Brother standing beside a very large Tree in the Blest Land of Eternal Springtime.

16-008 [_] **"A Sound Argument for Masters and Servants!"** (WHY Everyone Needs a Good Master, and every Master Needs Good Obedient Servants!) By The Worldwide People's Revolution!® Book 008. The Cover Photo shows a Pleasant Manmade Waterfalls.

16-009 [_] **"WHY are some Preachers so POOR?"** (HOW almost all Preachers could Get Moderately RICH, without Preaching any Outlandish LIES!) By The Worldwide People's Revolution!® Book 009. The Cover Photo shows a Portion of the Inside of a Gold-laden Church in the Blest Land of Eternal Springtime, worth a Billion Dollars!

(It is Time for some Sane Person to get Control of this Insane World!)

16-010 [_] "GOOD NEWS for REBEL WOMEN!" (HOW almost all Wives can become Moderately Rich without Leaving their Homes! Guaranteed!) By The Worldwide People's Revolution!® Book 010. The Cover Photo shows Beautiful Ceramic Work in the Blest Land of Eternal Springtime.

16-011 [_] "The Low Court of Supreme Injustices is Brought to Trial!" (The Worldwide People's Revolution Butts Heads with the United States Supreme Court, with or without their Black Robes of Hypocrisies and Lies!) By The Worldwide People's Revolution!® Book 011. The Cover Photo shows the United States Supreme Court Building in Washington.

16-012 [_] "The Right Design for Living!" (A List of Great Advantages for Building Beautiful Planned City States!) By The Worldwide People's Revolution!® Book 012. The Cover Photo shows the Great Pyramid at Chichen Itza, in Mexico.

16-013 [_] "The Gospel According to The Worldwide People's Revolution!" (The Good News from the Most Modern Perspective!) By The Worldwide People's Revolution!® Book 013. The Cover Photo shows a very Dirty Drunkard lying by the Street in the Cursed Land of Childish Rebellion, which does not Believe in Righteous Kings.

16-014 [_] "Poverty Hunger Riots Strikes Brutalities Election Deceptions and Civil Wars!" (The High Price that we Earthlings have Paid for Leaving the Good Land!) By The Worldwide People's Revolution!® Book 014. The Cover Photo shows Tombs in a Cemetery.

16-015 [_] "Seven Great Armies of Working Soldiers!" (HOW to Provide a Way for Everyone to WORK: so as to Eliminate Poverty, Crimes, Drug Abuses, Prisons and Unnecessary Taxes!) By The Worldwide People's Revolution!® Book 015. The Cover Photo shows a Truckload of Potential Working Soldiers.

16-016 [_] "The CONSTITUTION for the New RIGHTEOUS One-World GovernMint!" (HOW all Peoples can get True Justice, and Celebrate the Great Year of JUBILEE!) By The Worldwide People's Revolution!® Book 016. The Cover Photo shows a Gathering Thunderstorm.

16-017 [_] "The Great World TEMPLE of PEACE!" (The Glory of Jerusalem Arises Again!) By The Worldwide People's Revolution!® Book 017. The Cover Photo shows Old Jerusalem in all of its Naked and Potential Glory.

16-018 [_] "The Swanky Associations of Working Soldiers!" (A Fascinating Collection of Various Kinds of Voluntary Working Soldiers!) By The Worldwide People's Revolution!® Book 018. The Cover Photo shows a Beautiful Malachite Pyramid.

16-019 [_] "GLORIOUS Swanky Hotels Castles and Fortresses!" (Beautiful Planned City States for WISE Intelligent Well-Educated People with Common Sense and Good Understanding!) By The Worldwide People's Revolution!® Book 019. The Cover Photo shows a Beautiful "Million-dollar" Onyx Box in all of its Naked Glory.

16-020 [_] "Are you a Jobless Graduate of the SKQL uv FQLZ?" (HOW to Get a GOUD EJUKAASHUN without Robbing the Bank!) By The Worldwide People's Revolution!® Book 020. The Cover Photo shows a small and Beautiful Onyx Vase.

16-021 [_] "The LUSCIOUS All-Mineral Organic Method of Gardening!" (HOW to Grow DELICIOUS Satisfying Foods for Potential Kingz and Kweenz in Swanky PALACES!) By The Worldwide People's Revolution!® Book 021. The Cover Photo shows Beautiful Green Terraces in the Blest Land of Eternal Summertime.

16-022 [_] "Did God or Satan Ordain Medical Doctors??" (Ask Huck Finn and/or Nigger Jim: because neither Tom Sawyer nor Judge Thatcher would Know!) By The Worldwide People's Revolution!® Book 022. The Cover Photo shows Pretty Flowers at a Tomb.

16-023 [_] "The BIG White OUTHOUSE on the Not-so-Biblical Capitol DUNGHILL!" (The Chief Sins of the Divided States of United Lies!) By The Worldwide People's Revolution!® Book 023. The Cover Photo shows the Capitol Building in Washington, District of Criminals, District of Confusion, District of Colombian Drug Addicts, etc., etc.

16-024 [_] "The Public School of IGNERUNT FQLZ!" (HOW we have been GRAATLEE DISEEVD!) By The Worldwide People's Revolution!® Book 024. The Cover Photo shows a Disorganized Fruit Market in a City of Confusion.

16-025 [_] "In thu Beeginingz uv Thingz!" (Thu Kreeaashun Stooree frum thu Beegining!) By The Worldwide People's Revolution!® Book 025. The Cover Photo shows a Yellow Sapote, which not one Person in a Million has ever Tasted, in spite of being one of the most Pleasant Sweetest Fruits known to Mankind, which does not Ship very well, which must Ripen on the Tree, in order to be Extremely GOOD, as in "Heavenly Good!"

16-026 [_] "God Speaks and the Whole World Listens!" (Fire on the Mountain from the Burning Bush by the Spirit of Truth!) By The Worldwide People's Revolution!® Book 026. The Cover Photo shows the Sign or Flag for "The New RIGHTEOUS One-World Government!"

16-027 [_] "Does a Good Soldier have to be a MURDERER?" (Seven Great Swanky Armies of Voluntary Working Soldiers!) By The Worldwide People's Revolution!® Book 027. Dan.

16-028 [_] "Thu Nq MAGNUFIID Verzhun uv Thu PROVERBZ uv KING SOLUMUN in Plaan Ingglish!" (The Understandable Version of the Famous Proverbs of King Solomon in Plain English!) By The Worldwide People's Revolution!® Book 028. The Cover Photo shows Gemstones in an Onyx Jewelry Box.

16-029 [_] "UNLIMITED ENERJEE 99 Percent Pollutions Free!" (HOW to Obtain FREE ElecTrickery, Worldwide!) By The Worldwide People's Revolution!® Book 029. The Cover Photo shows an Onyx Tray for a large Spoon in the Kitchen.

16-030 [_] "FREEDUM uv SPEECH!" (U Speshoul Maguzeen uv Onust Upinyunz!) By The Worldwide People's Revolution!® Book 030-0001. The Cover Photo shows a Portion of

(It is Time for some Sane Person to get Control of this Insane World!)

one of the Author's Marble Countertops, worth 100$ per square foot, for an Example of what you could also have, if you Exercise your Faith, Hope, Trust, Love, Patience, Persistence, and OBEDIENCE!

16-031 [_] **"A Sure Cure for GUN VIOLENCE!" (HOW TO STOP GANG WARS and CRIMINAL SHOOTINGS!) By The Worldwide People's Revolution!®** Book 031. The Cover Photo shows a Short Shotgun, which is fully loaded and ready for any Tax Master who might Attempt to Steel the Retirement Home, who never moved a Finger to Help Build it, whose Anti-Christ False Federal Cover-up WICKED Government allowed Banksters to Rob us of 30 Years of Hard Work and 300,000+ dollars-worth of Investments in our Uncommon American Farm. (Future Books will have Cover Photos of some of that Hard Work. Please be Patient.)

16-032 [_] **"AIIRMWVC and Reasonable Solutions!" (Aliens, Illegal Immigrants, Refugees, Migrant Workers and other Victims of Capitalism!) By The Worldwide People's Revolution!®** Book 032. The Cover Photo shows a "Sea of People."

16-033 [_] **"Mark Twain Races for the PRESIDENCY!" (The 2016 Presidential Candidates Desperately Need Some STRONG Undefeatable COMPETITION!) By The Worldwide People's Revolution!®** Book 033. The Cover Photo shows a Mountain Goat and a Silver Dollar.

16-034 [_] **"ECCLESIASTES UNCOVERED!" (The New MAGNIFIED Version of Ecclesiastes and the Song of Solomon in Plain English!) By The Worldwide People's Revolution!®** Book 034. The Cover Photo shows a Peacock Resting.

16-035 [_] **"The Environmentalists' Paradise!" (HOW almost Everyone could be Living in a Beautiful Manmade Paradise!) By The Worldwide People's Revolution!®** Book 035. The Cover Photo shows an Artist's Conception of Paradise for a single Family in the Blest Land of Perfect Oneness, where all is at Peace.

16-036 [_] **"The Seven Basic Spiritual Building Blocks of LIFE!" (Faith Hope Trust Love Patience Persistence and Obedience!) By The Worldwide People's Revolution!®** Book 036. The Cover Photo shows Onion Domes trimmed with Gold.

16-037 [_] **"DIETS!" (A Reasonable Solution for the "Eternal Controversy"!) By The Worldwide People's Revolution!®** Book 037. The Cover Photo shows some Colorful Fruits.

16-038 [_] **"The Nature of CAPITALISM!" (A List of the EVILS of CAPITALISM!) By The Worldwide People's Revolution!®** Book 038. The Cover Photo shows a Pretty Red Car.

16-039 [_] **"SWANGKEENOMIKS Rules the Roost!" (HOW all People can Prosper in a RIIT WAA, and STOP Polluting the Earth with Capitalist TRASH!) By The Worldwide People's Revolution!®** Book 039. The Cover Photo shows a small Portion of our Retirement Home before the 5,000+ square-foot Roof was Installed.

16-040 [_] **"The New MAGNIFIED Version of The Book of MOORMUN!" (The Story of the White and Dark Indians in the Americas!) By The Worldwide People's Revolution!®** Book 040, Volumes 1 and 2. The Cover Photos show the Queen of England's Golden Coach, and one of our Marbleous Spanish Walls, which is worth a thousand dollars per square Yard, installed on 7 similar Walls, which are 12 feet long. It is very Inspiring. No one could Study it for very long without Believing in a Great Creator God.

16-041 [_] "The Great Worldwide TELEVISED Court HEARING!" (That Great Meeting of the Most Intelligent Minds!) By The Worldwide People's Revolution!® Book 041. The Cover Photo shows Mount Popotits covered with Snow.

16-042 [_] "The Secret City of the Great King!" (HOW the True Church will Escape from the Great Tribulation!) By The Worldwide People's Revolution!® Book 042. The Cover Photo shows a Colorful Ferris Wheel. P-5877.

16-043 [_] "Terrorists Beware that your Days are Numbered!" (HOW to Bring those Terrorist Attacks to a Screeching HALT!) By The Worldwide People's Revolution!® Book 043. The Cover Photo shows a Picture of George Warmonger Bush. This Book also contains the Fascinating Book of LEHI.

16-044 [_] "The New MAGNIFIED Version of ISAIAH in Plain English!" (The Understandable Version of the Book of Isaiah!) By The Worldwide People's Revolution!® Book 044. The Cover Photo shows a Swanky Potato / Avocado Salad with Sweet Peas and Corn.

16-045 [_] "HOW to Become a HOLY Man!" (40 Good Reasons WHY People Should FAST and PRAY!) By The Worldwide People's Revolution!® Book 045. The Cover Photo will show a Holy Man, just as soon as one Presents himself for the Photograph.

16-046 [_] "The Proper RULES for FASTING!" (The Complete Instruction Manual for True Repentance!) By The Worldwide People's Revolution!® Book 046. The Cover Photo shows an Unclean Man.

16-047 [_] "Are Americans the Most STUPID People who ever Lived?" (HOW Working People can PROSPER and Live in PEACE Under the Rulership of a RIGHTEOUS KING!) By The Worldwide People's Revolution!® Book 047. The Cover Photo shows a large Portion of the Author's Marbleous Living Room Floor, which is worth 100,000$.

16-048 [_] "An Amazing Collection of Wit and Wisdom!" (The Marvelous Tale of the Colorful Peacock from Angel Ridge, and the Strong Rope of Hope!) By The Worldwide People's Revolution!® Book 048. The Cover Photo shows a Book Display.

16-049 [_] "Justifications for Capitalizations!" (WHY The Worldwide People's Revolution!® Defies the School of Fools by Capitalizing Love and Hate!) By The Worldwide People's Revolution!® Book 049. The Cover Photo shows a Water Tower.

16-050 [_] "The END of CONFUSION!" (The Great CELEBRATION of the Magnificent Wedding of the Humble Honest Nations, and the Grand Year of JUBILEE!) By The Worldwide People's Revolution!® Book 050. The Cover Photo shows a Portion of a Colorful Parade.

(It is Time for some Sane Person to get Control of this Insane World!)

16-051 [_] "**The Loathsome Burdens of the Independent Jackasses!**" (A New Approach for Solving our Massive Problems!) **By The Worldwide People's Revolution!® Book 051.** The Cover Photo shows a Spanish Military Barracks.

16-052 [_] "**Are we Tax Slaves of a Lower Order than Lying Red JEWS?**" (HOW to be Liberated from all Slavery, Worldwide!) **By The Worldwide People's Revolution!® Book 052.** The Cover Photo shows a few Tax Slaves.

16-053 [_] "**The Great False Economy is now DEBUNKED!**" (Adolf Hitler had a much Better Economic System!) **By The Worldwide People's Revolution!® Book 053.** The Cover Photo shows a Capitalist Toilet Brush.

16-054 [_] "**The UGLY Scarred Dishonest Face of Poor Old Miserable UNCLE SAM!**" (A Memorial Day Legacy!) **By The Worldwide People's Revolution!® Book 054.** The Cover Photo shows a Poster of "Uncle Sam," who Symbolizes the Federal Government of **"The Divided States of United Lies!"**

16-055 [_] "**The United States of the Whole World!**" (A True Global Economy for the Masses of Working People!) **By The Worldwide People's Revolution!® Book 055.** A Photo of a 110-year-old Well-made Mexican Rocking Chair with a Cowhide Seat.

16-056 [_] "**The New RIGHTEOUS One-World Government!**" (HOW to Establish a Righteous One-World Government without Going to WAR!) **By The Worldwide People's Revolution!® Book 056.** The Cover Photo shows the Flag of that Good Government.

16-057 [_] "**Those Ridiculous Contradictions within the Holy Bible!**" (HOW to Read the Bible with an Open Mind!) **By The Worldwide People's Revolution!® Book 057.** The Cover Photo shows a Purple Tree.

16-058 [_] "**The Divided States of United Lies!**" (The so-called "United States of North America," in Disguise!) **By The Worldwide People's Revolution!® Book 058.** The Cover Photo shows a Map of the United States.

16-059 [_] "**The Complete SURVEYS of our VALUES!**" (SURVEYS of Religious Spiritual Political Governmental Sexual Social Moral Economic Business Labor Habitual and Miscellaneous VALUES! **By The Worldwide People's Revolution!® Book 059.** The Cover Photo shows a Large Onyx Vase in the Author's Palace.

16-060 [_] "**HOW to Get our PRIORITIES in ORDER!**" (The Glories of Democracy; and, Does DEMON-ocracy have its Priorities in Order?) **By The Worldwide People's Revolution!® Book 060.** The Cover Photo shows a Different View of that Large Onyx Vase.

16-061 [_] "**The New MAGNIFIED Version of the GOOD NEWS According to Saint LUKE!**" (The Magnified Gospel of Luke in Plain English!) **By The Worldwide People's Revolution!® Book 061.** The Cover Photo shows Agate Windows.

16-062 [_] "The New MAGNIFIED Version of the GOOD NEWS According to Saint JOHN!" (The Gospel According to Saint John Zebedee Boanerges in Plain English!) By The Worldwide People's Revolution!® Book 062. The Cover Photo shows the Parthenon.

16-063 [_] "The New MAGNIFIED Version of the Book of ACTS!" (The Understandable Version of the ACTS of the Apostles in Plain English!) By The Worldwide People's Revolution!® Book 063. The Cover Photo shows a Small Portion of Arches National Park.

16-064 [_] "The New MAGNIFIED Version of the PSALMS of King David!" (The Understandable Version of the Famous Psalms in Plain English!) By The Worldwide People's Revolution!® Book 064. The Cover Photo shows some of the Grand Canyon.

16-065 [_] "A List of FAIR Swanky Wages!" (The Equitable Wage System!) By The Worldwide People's Revolution!® Book 065. The Cover Photo shows a Pile of Money.

16-066 [_] "Beautiful Swanky PALACES!" (A New Concept in Living Habits!) By The Worldwide People's Revolution!® Book 066. The Cover Photo shows a Bouquet of Pretty Flowers in the Author's Kitchen.

16-067 [_] "The Swanky Sword of Divine Truths!" (The Most Powerful Weapon in the Whole Universe!) By The Worldwide People's Revolution!® Book 067. The Cover Photo a Robe beside a Split Sword at the bottom of the Photo.

16-068 [_] "Has your Life become Extremely Complicated?" (HOW to Live a SIMPLE Life!) By The Worldwide People's Revolution!® Book 068. The Cover Photo shows a Horse.

16-069 [_] "The IDEAL Place to Live!" (HOW to Discover the Ideal Place to Live!) By The Worldwide People's Revolution!® Book 069. The Cover Photo shows an Ideal Place to Live!

16-070 [_] "Our Elected King Who Speaks Out!" (It is Time for some Sane Person to get Control of this Insane World!) By The Worldwide People's Revolution!® Book 070. The Cover Photo shows a Photo of an Eagle's View of New York City from the Top of the Empire State Building.

16-071 [_] "How GAY is GOD?" (Oh the Wonders of it all when it ALL Hangs Out!) By The Worldwide People's Revolution!® Book 071. The Cover shows a Photo of 2 Gay Dogs.

{NOTE: This List of Available Books will be Updated Periodically. If you fail to find any of these Books on Amazon.com, just be Patient: because I am a One-Man Army, you might say. All of the Books are written, and just need to be Posted, after they are Updated.}

www.ingramcontent.com/pod-product-compliance
Lightning Source LLC
Chambersburg PA
CBHW080712190526
45169CB00006B/2342